FIVE PATHWAYS TO WHOLENESS

FIVE PATHWAYS
TO WHOLENESS

*Explorations in pastoral care
and counselling*

Roger Hurding

First published in Great Britain in 2013

Society for Promoting Christian Knowledge
36 Causton Street
London SW1P 4ST
www.spckpublishing.co.uk

British Library Cataloguing-in-Publication Data
A catalogue record for this book is available from the British Library

ISBN 978–0–281–07036–7
eBook ISBN 978–0–281–07037–4

Typeset by Graphicraft Limited, Hong Kong
First printed in Great Britain by Ashford Colour Press
Subsequently digitally printed in Great Britain

eBook by Graphicraft Limited, Hong Kong

Produced on paper from sustainable forests

To Joy and our much loved grandchildren:
Luke, Verity, Ruth, Maya, Ciara and Ethan

Contents

Foreword by the Revd David Runcorn   ix

Preface   xiii

1   The journey charted   1

2   Biblical counselling: the transformed mind   23

3   Healing ministries: the forward gain   41

4   Pastoral counselling: the maturing person   66

5   Spiritual direction: the uncomplicated heart   88

6   Social change: the reformed community   110

7   Five pathways, one hope   130

Notes   143

Select bibliography and further reading   160

Index of biblical references   167

Index of names   168

Index of subjects   171

Foreword: mind the gap

'Life is not simple, nor love inevitable,' wrote novelist Niall Williams.[1] Not that we need telling. We already know this to our cost and frustration. The search for what we hope will bring happiness, fulfilment and what we mean by 'wholeness' is anything but straightforward. Cul-de-sacs and wrong turns abound. But we are nothing if not determined. The greater part of life in our Western world is shaped around the endless pursuit of this.

We do our living in the gap between the world we find ourselves in and the one we long for. We never quite lose a restless sense, deep down, that what we are is not who we *truly* are and that what we are *not* is who we truly *are*. In fact, we learn this from the earliest stories of childhood. All those ugly ducklings who were actually beautiful swans; the scullery maids who were really the king's true love; the toads who were handsome princes. All that life trapped under a spell of lost or stolen identity, waiting for the release of one whose kiss is true.[2]

This means that alongside the pursuit of our desires and dreams of wholeness, we must build relationships with our frustrations, pain and incompleteness. Finding a place to start is itself a challenge. It may be the single least helpful feature of our world that, at the press of a button, *everything* is accessible from *anywhere*. There is a kind of rootless vagrancy about the way we pursue what we need in life. If we seem to get nowhere it may be because we struggle to start from *some*where. Psychotherapist Adam Philips describes a society that lives 'on the compass of our excitement'. That leaves us endlessly reactive to the latest distraction or stimulation. The cost of this is everywhere apparent. And do we even know how exploited this leaves us? Life comes marked by high levels of anxiety, dis-ease and varieties of consumptive disorders. The result is profoundly dehumanizing. But a world driven by technology approaches our pain as a 'problem' to be 'solved', while a culture shaped around markets only really knows how to approach 'wholeness', like happiness, as a consumer product – for those who can afford it.

Into such a raw context of confusion and need this book lays out the foundations of the Christian understanding of wholeness and explores the pathways that lead there. And what does this word 'wholeness' *not* include? It certainly contains much more than we usually allow it to. Hurding is a compassionate but probing observer of human journeying, within and beyond Christian faith. No pathway is allowed to become narrowed to private ends. Rather the word grows with the telling. One of the most challenging chapters explores the social understanding of 'wholeness', including reflections on multicultural society, gender relationships and the deepening crisis of global ecology.

A significant feature of this book is the careful attention Hurding pays to history. The development of therapies, beliefs and approaches to wholeness are all carefully traced, set in their historical context and critically evaluated. There is important wisdom here. To know where we are and where we need to be going, we must pay attention to where we have come from. Pathways to wholeness (rather than poorly mapped trails of fleeting therapeutic fashions) will always be a work of remembrance. That is the reason the Bible gives such priority to the work of remembering. As Hurding himself knows well, a good counsellor or guide will always be a careful historian. So he offers clear and accessible maps that trace the very varied approaches to human healing and flourishing, sets them in their contexts and guides us in reading them critically for their gifts and their shortcomings.

Another quality of this book is the place of people in it. Very early in the book, Hurding notes that however clear the map it is no substitute for actually making the journey. There is no theory in this book that is not found embedded in lived experience. And this is core to the Christian approaches to wholeness. The word 'wholeness' always take flesh. So people and their stories weave their own pathways throughout this book. Hurding's evident care for the people he has listened to for so long reminds me of a counsellor who would call someone's story their 'personal holy scripture'. It must be received with reverence and respect – as something holy – not least because the Christian conviction is that God's grace weaves pathways, known or unknown, in the depths.

Finally, this is an exploration of human and Christian wholeness by someone who has lived with long-term, often critical, health problems.

'Wholeness' by any popular understanding of the word has eluded him. Hurding knows from personal experience that 'wholeness' is not a problem to be solved. Nor is it available over the counter. He writes with the gentle patience of one who knows that even the most urgent questions of life need to be asked slowly and cannot be forced into quick answers. I think he would approve of Raymond Carver's asking himself whether he has found what he wanted from life. Yes, he says. And what was that? 'To feel myself beloved on the earth'.[3] The heart of Christian wholeness is found here. And if that is true, then, because 'we love confusedly, we fallen ones', 'the journey of life is for setting love in order' (p. 3).

Hurding begins the book by talking about his boyhood love of maps. Map-making is a work of painstaking observation and careful exploring. Such is this book. It is a loving, faithful exercise in charting the complex and uneven terrain of human living, believing and relating. There is only one thing better than being given a map for a journey. It is to have an experienced, wise guide to make the journey with. And that is what we are offered in these pages.

David Runcorn

Preface

A conversation in the summer of 2012 with John Turner, colleague, friend and former Director of Network Counselling in Bristol stirred me into approaching SPCK with a project for a new book. To my delight, Lauren Zimmerman, Alison Barr and their fellow editors responded enthusiastically to the synopsis and sample chapters of *Five Pathways to Wholeness*.

I have taken elements of the outline of Part II of an earlier book, *Pathways to Wholeness*, and revised, updated and rewritten the material. This has proved to be a most rewarding experience. Ironically, my desire to offer more on what it means to journey towards wholeness has been fraught with personal health problems, including frequent angina and breathlessness, in spite of a quadruple bypass in 1993, as well as the aftermath of chronic brucellosis, an undulating flu-like condition, the struggles with long-term diabetes and progressive renal failure.

Looking back through over 50 years since qualifying as a doctor in 1959, it is good to remember and acknowledge the many influences that have shaped my thinking and practice. Within general practice during the 1960s, I became committed to offering 'long appointments' to some of my more depressed and anxious patients, following the psychoanalytic approach fostered by Michael and Enid Balint at London's Tavistock Clinic. In my work as a student health doctor at the University of Bristol in the 1970s, my prime specialist commitment was to spend most weekday afternoons counselling students, engaging with an array of problems, including identity crises, exam nerves, difficulties in relating, struggles with gender issues, depression, anxiety, psychotic breakdown and drug addictions. Also during the 1970s, I worked in psychotherapy in the Department of Mental Health's outpatients and then, on through into the 1980s, I attended a number of workshops in transactional analysis, psychodrama, family therapy and client-centred psychotherapy. This included a stretch of blindness over two years, a complication of diabetes, which forced my retirement from student health. This was a time of huge readjustment, discovering an unexpected value in attending training workshops with my good psychiatric friend Richard Winter. On one memorable Saturday he and I were the only men along with about 50 women engaging with a 'hands-on' day of psychodrama. Much of the role-play in small groups proved hilarious as I stumbled round the hall within my band of friendly, supportive women, none of whom I had previously met.

Another important influence on my approach to counselling and psychotherapy in the 1970s was the Christians in Psychiatry group, under the aegis of Monty Barker, consultant psychiatrist in Bristol. Here, a lively gathering of psychiatrists, social workers and counsellors met to debate current issues in our respective professions. Psychiatric colleagues from this group included Glynn Harrison, Jan Truscott and Richard Winter.

Further, during the early 1980s, once I had been obliged to leave student health, I became involved with Care and Counsel in London, one of the first Christian counselling organizations to form during that period. A group of us met regularly, at first in London then later in Oxford, to discuss the burgeoning interest in the integration of theology and psychology. This nexus became good friends and included David Atkinson, Myra Chave-Jones, Joy Guy, John Hall, Richard Winter, Liz Shedden and Roger Moss. At that time we pioneered a series of weekend workshops on the integrationist theme. The first of these was based at the London Bible College in 1983 and then at Trinity College in Bristol in 1985, moving on to biennial conferences at The Hayes, Swanwick, Derbyshire, beginning in 1987, where clergy, counsellors, psychotherapists, psychologists, social workers, pastoral carers and spiritual directors met, discussed, prayed and worshipped together. These conferences continue to this day under the title of 'Continuing the Journey'; the latest, in the spring of 2012, was on the theme of 'Minding the gaps: finding edges, holding tensions', in which 'those things which divide as well as unite us – issues of difference and similarity, individuality and community, separateness and connection' were explored.

Largely inspired by my years with Care and Counsel and involvement with the early Swanwick conferences, I contributed to the setting up of Network Counselling in Bristol, launching its first training programme in 1986, under the directorship of David Mitchell. Now known as Network Counselling and Training, this organization still prospers, offering professional counselling and university-validated courses in counsellor training, being affiliated to the British Association for Counselling and Psychotherapy and the Association for Christian Counsellors.

Also in the 1980s, I attended university-based conferences in pastoral studies, learning from, among others, the practical theologians Elaine Graham, Don Browning, Paul Ballard, Stephen Pattison and David Lyall. In the early 1990s, I trained and became qualified as a registered user of the Myers-Briggs® Type Indicator and also engaged with a course of training in spiritual direction.

In 1980 I started as a visiting lecturer in pastoral care and counselling at Trinity College in Bristol, and in time I was able to extend my commitment there to take a Masters' class in pastoral theology. I finally retired from the college in 2000. During these 20 years I greatly valued the inspiration and encouragement of a number of colleagues, including John Wesson, John Bimson, David Gillett, Jackie Searle and David Runcorn.

I would also like to express my thanks for the gracious support of David Runcorn, in writing the Foreword to this book, Wendy Bryant, and the clergy team here in Portishead – Andy Bryant, Christine Judson, Tina Hodgett and Jeremy Putnam. These have been generous with their time to Joy and me during this more restricted stage of our lives. There are others, too, I would like to thank, those whose identities have been obscured for the sake of confidentiality, who have helped directly and indirectly with this book's gestation.

I am very grateful to Alison Barr, my editor at SPCK. She has been most helpful and affirming in her advice and a pleasure to work with. I express my gratitude, too, to my other editors at SPCK, to Lauren Zimmerman and Rima Devereaux, as well as my copy-editor, Kathryn Wolfendale.

Finally, I give a very warm thank you to Joy for her patience, love and encouragement amid my preoccupations in writing this new book.

1

The journey charted

The need to create reliable cognitive maps of the world has been carried to the point where the person prefers the map to the territory, the menu to the meal, the model to the reality.

(David W. Augsburger)[1]

As a child and a teenager I was greatly intrigued by maps and map-making and learned to read the contours and symbols with delight, thus visualizing the territory. At times, though, a particular map proved inadequate for the reality of a landscape. In my teen years a much-loved cousin and I cycled and camped in, to us, an unexplored part of mid-Essex, relying on an old map of the area. Imagine our surprise when, topping a hill, we faced what looked like a large inland sea spread before us, inundating the hedgerows and fields that our map depicted. This proved to be Abberton Reservoir, constructed in the years since the map was printed and, once discovered, a favourite haunt for my early birdwatching years.

It is a tendency in our modern world to systematize, categorize and try to make maps that seek to unscramble the complexities of everyday life. In seeking to chart our journey into wholeness we need to take heed of David Augsburger's words given at the head of this chapter, in which he points out the folly of preferring 'the map to the territory', akin to favouring a menu over the rich sensations of enjoying a good meal, or of celebrating, say, a Dinky model of a vintage car more than the real thing. In seeking to delineate five pathways in our Christian journeying, we need to remember that the realities and complexities of what it means to be human will always question and challenge the simplifications of our cognitive maps.

Even so, the most fundamental point to make as we begin to chart the way forward is to say that we need others on life's journey – not only in that our sense of personal identity is defined by our relationships, but that to learn to be truly human necessitates, at least from time to time, the value of another or others to guide, support and encourage us. Here we are in the heartland of the New Testament's injunctions towards 'one-anotherness': 'Outdo one another in showing honour' (Rom. 12.10); 'Instruct one another' (Rom. 15.14); 'Be kind to one another . . . forgiving one another' (Eph. 4.32); 'Bear one another's burdens' (Gal. 6.2); 'Love one another with mutual affection' (Rom. 12.10).

And so, as we shape our map of pathways to wholeness we will keep in mind the formative part that the Bible plays in the story of the Church's care for others. That has been the case throughout Christianity's history, but there is now a fresh impetus to discern the place of Scripture in the Church's response to human need. As Herbert Anderson puts it in *The Bible in Pastoral Practice*:

> New perspectives on interpreting the Bible and new approaches to pastoral care promise new possibilities for connecting the Bible and pastoral care in authentic ways. At the same time, there is a new awareness that pastoral care is ideally situated to answer the vital connection between the Bible and the moral dilemmas of our time.[2]

We will consider our way forward under three main headings: first, pastoral care, which is, as it were, the very landscape that we seek to map; followed by a pastoral theological method, giving us the tools for both our map-making and engagement with the terrain; and finally mapping the pathways, in which we will focus on the key to the ensuing map in terms of, for example, the use of Scripture, metaphor and spirituality.

Pastoral care

Margaret,[3] in her mid-forties, came to see me in an agitated state to say that her husband Colin was physically and verbally violent towards her and their two boys, Simon and Andrew, now in their teens. Margaret and Colin were members of their local church and had, for a while, taught in one of the children's Bible classes. Under sufferance, Colin had agreed to go with Margaret to see their curate, but when challenged about his vindictiveness towards his wife he had been 'livid, and walked out'. They had also been to a nearby Christian counselling service but, once again, Colin gave up on the interviews, leaving Margaret to attend by herself. In the light of all this, Tessa, another member of the same church, had encouraged Margaret to see me for advice.

Margaret declared that Colin 'will brook no contradiction' from her or the boys. Recently, Simon and Andrew had begun to express independent views and their father 'saw red'. Andrew, the younger of the brothers, had begun to show hatred towards his father.

What place does pastoral care have in this story? Here there is a network of caring within a church and para-church context. The curate, Tessa and the Christian counsellor who supported Margaret, all played their part. My own comparatively brief advisory role entailed a liaison with her counsellor, seeking the possibility of family therapy for Margaret and the boys, and a discussion with her concerning her need to see a solicitor in the face of Colin's violence.

The notion of pastoral care is as old as human need and the calling to respond to that need. Within the Judaeo-Christian tradition the impetus to care for others lies in the revealed nature of Yahweh – who 'defends the cause of the fatherless and the widow, and loves the alien' (Deut. 10.18, NIV) – and the unfolding perception of God as Trinity, three persons within the one godhead, interrelating in perfect love and calling the emerging Church to respond to the summary of the 'entire law': 'Love your neighbour as yourself' (Gal. 5.14). This neigh-bourly love is to be all-inclusive, boundary-crossing and tailored to precise human predicament: Jesus urges his followers to love their enemies; he exemplifies a love that breaks Judaic taboos towards Samaritans, women, children and work, even healing work, on the Sabbath; and he challenges God's people to respond to the communal needs of hunger, thirst, homelessness, lack of clothing, sickness and imprisonment. It goes without saying that such wide-sweeping com-passion includes within its compass love towards family, friends and fellow believers – the last, at times, the most difficult to love, since there may be little or no 'natural' affection involved. Leanne Payne is realistic about the high calling of Christian love when she writes, 'We love confusedly, we fallen ones; the journey of life is for setting love in order.'[4]

It would be incorrect, though, to equate Christian love with pastoral care, as the latter is simply one manifestation of that love. Perhaps one of the most helpful ways of visualizing the essence of pastoral care in biblical terms is to see its close links with the Greek word *paraklesis* – exhortation, encouragement, comfort, consolation. Jacob Firet takes this term as part of a threefold picture of 'pastoral role-fulfilment', comprising proclamation (*kerygma*), teaching (*didache*) and pastoral care (*paraklesis*). These three pastoral 'modes' are clearly interrelated, so Firet argues, and yet there is in the parakletic ministry something 'which lies in a different sphere from that of the authoritative proclamation of salvation and the didactic unfolding of it'.[5] He sums up this pastoral calling in these words: 'paraklesis is the mode in which God comes to people in their situations of dread, suffering, sin, despair, error, and insufficiency', bringing them into 'the joy of new obedience' and a readiness 'to fulfil special tasks within the body of Christ'.[6]

We can look more closely at this transformative work by posing two questions: 'What is pastoral care?' and 'Does it need an *underlying theology*?' In Chapter 4, we will ask, 'Why *pastoral* care?' as we examine the links between the metaphor of the shepherd and pastoral care and counselling.

What is pastoral care?

From ancient times pastoral care has been simply what Christians do as part of their neighbourly love towards needy fellow human beings. Although great stretches of the history of pastoral care have invested the shepherding role[7] in that of the ordained minister, the thread of the 'priesthood of all believers', however tenuous at times, has also run throughout the centuries – to free women as well as men, laity as well as clergy, to respond to the call to care for others in the name of Christ. Since it is modernity's bid to analyse, define and systematize, it is only in comparatively recent times that attempts have been made to clarify a precise understanding of pastoral care. We will consider two definitions.

The first, by William A. Clebsch and Charles R. Jaekle, though published in 1964, has become a classic that is referred back to even in the most recent attempts to define pastoral care:[8]

> The ministry of the cure of souls, or pastoral care, consists of helping acts, done by representative Christian persons, directed toward the healing, sustaining, guiding, and reconciling of troubled

persons whose troubles arise in the context of ultimate meanings and concerns.[9]

Although this definition has been criticized by Stephen Pattison for its apparent clericalism ('representative Christian persons'), individualism ('troubled persons') and problem-centredness (focus on 'troubles'), it is worth drawing out two of its clauses for constructive comment.

The overall division of historic pastoral care into 'healing, sustaining, guiding, and reconciling'[10] has a pragmatic usefulness in terms of an understanding of the rich inheritance of *cura animarum* – the cure of souls – to use an established alternative term. I used this analysis many times in discussions with theological students and found that the four functions of care resonate well with recent debates on pastoral issues: for example, the relationship between a theology of healing and a theology of suffering (these two subsumed in Clebsch and Jaekle's 'healing' and 'sustaining' functions respectively); between pastoral counselling and spiritual direction (under 'guiding'); and around notions of forgiveness and church discipline (under 'reconciling'). This fourfold structure is a valuable contribution towards the map-making enterprise of this book.

Clebsch and Jaekle's notion of 'representative Christian persons' is more open to misunderstanding in the light of the current debate on pastoral care. There is a tendency in the North American scene to equate the 'pastoral' with the 'clerical', whereas in a British context, although that view is still represented, pastoral care and counselling are generally regarded as the potential province for *all* Christian carers. In fact, Clebsch and Jaekle adopt an 'in-between' position, seeing their 'representative persons' as people 'who, either *de jure* or *de facto*, bring to bear upon human troubles the resources, the wisdom, and the authority of Christian faith and life'. Although such individuals 'commonly' hold 'the office of authorized pastors', they may possess 'no churchly office whatever'. Either way, Clebsch and Jaekle seem to argue, the local church is safeguarded from the well-intentioned but wayward ministrations of the inept and self-authorized by, among other things, the possession and exercise of 'the authority of a company of Christian believers'.[11] Whereas Pattison is right to criticize them for their individualism, Clebsch and Jaekle clearly also see pastoral care in a communal and corporate Christian context.

The second definition, by David Lyall, is among more recent attempts to give an understanding of pastoral care. Lyall, in his *Integrity of Pastoral Care* (2001), acknowledges the difficulty in making a simple defining statement of such a diffuse calling, since pastoral care can be seen at a range of levels, from the care offered by clergy and laity in a church context, through comparable attention to need in classroom or college, to simple neighbourly care offered on a daily basis. He therefore gives a number of parameters for pastoral care, including:

> Pastoral care involves the establishment of a relationship or relationships whose purpose may encompass support in a time of trouble and personal and/or spiritual growth through deeper understanding of oneself, others and/or God. Pastoral care will have at its heart the affirmation of meaning and worth of persons and will endeavour to strengthen their ability to respond creatively to whatever life brings.[12]

Here is a definition that accords well with the anguish that Margaret faced when confronted by Colin's short fuse and angry outbursts. For her curate, Tessa, other church members and her counsellor, relationships were established that offered support and sought to help her to a deeper understanding of herself, her husband and, hopefully, God. For example, counselling helped her reflect on her own upbringing, in which her mother criticized her for her lack of boyfriends; in response to this, Margaret signed on with a dating agency and visited nightclubs, rather desperately seeking male contact. Eventually she met Colin, ten years older and divorced from his first marriage. At the age of 30 she married him, 'to make a go' of the relationship. She also discussed, in counselling, the fact that Colin's father had deserted his mother when he was still at primary school and that Colin had experienced very little affirmation and warmth from his mother. Here she began to discern something of the factors that had contributed towards his controlling manner. Her pastoral carers in their turn encouraged Margaret, in spite of her huge struggles, not to give up on her various church commitments. Hopefully, through the counselling process, the support of her church, the potential of family therapy for her and her boys, and an interview with a solicitor, Margaret was able to begin 'to respond creatively to whatever life brings'.

An underlying theology

In what way, if any, might an underlying theology affect the outcomes of pastoral care for Margaret, Colin, Simon and Andrew? Surely their prime need is for good listening, compassion, wise advice, support and, where necessary, challenge and confrontation. Where does theology fit into the very human dilemmas and confusions of their daily struggle?

Gordon Lynch, in *Pastoral Care and Counselling*, writes that values 'provide the compass bearings by which we make sense of and judge pastoral practice',[13] and since my approach to pastoral care is within the context of the Church, we need to examine the place of Christian theology in establishing our compass bearing towards wholeness.

Historically, pastoral care has often been diffident, and even coy, about claiming a need for an underlying theology. Its emphasis has been intensely practical and the idea of theologizing in the face of an anguished request for guidance, the deep unsettlement of caring for a loved one with Alzheimer's, the last words of a dying parishioner or the weeping of a grieving relative has often been far from the intentions of the sensitive pastor. Perhaps something of Brueggemann's thought hovers at the back of our minds: 'The serpent is the first in the Bible to seem knowing and critical about God and to practice *theology* in the place of *obedience*.'[14]

But all this sidestepping of theology can be seen as a failure of nerve, since, to quote David Tracy, 'all our experience, indeed all praxis, is theory-laden',[15] and pastoral care, a ministry of frontline experience, is as 'theory-laden' as any other human enterprise. Elsewhere, Tracy declares that '*praxis* is correctly understood as the critical relationship between theory and practice whereby each is dialectically influenced and transformed by the other'.[16] And this, surely, is the heart of the matter for pastoral care, since its theology, as with all theology, needs to demonstrate the critical interface between theory and practice: a praxis in which theory is shown forth in enlightened practice and practice informs theory with the cutting edge of everyday life. To reflect on the anguish and distress of a young woman dying of cancer, as I have had to do, to be angry with God and face unanswerable questions, and then to return to the bedside to make some feeble attempt at companionship in suffering, is about *doing* theology – a pastoral theology that is praxis. This is where Colin

Morris had it right, when he said, 'Your theology is what you are when the talking stops and the action starts.'

Given that theology, at its best, has hands and feet that lead to practical action, we also need to see where that practical theology fits within the scheme of things.

Practical and pastoral theology

Traditionally, theology can be subdivided into **fundamental theology**, addressing such foundations of the faith as the existence of God and the nature of revelation; **systematic theology**, the attempt to give shape and pattern to the detailed content of Christian belief; and **practical theology**, comprising such 'ministerial activities' as preaching, teaching and pastoral care.

In the Europe of the late eighteenth century, practical theology began to emerge as a feature in the curriculum of academic theology. Throughout the next two centuries, practical theology was caught up in an essentially pragmatic approach to human need, in which its offspring, **pastoral theology**, was seen as simply the province of a theological reflection that undergirded the 'activities' of pastoral care. Stephen Pattison and James Woodward, in *The Blackwell Reader in Pastoral and Practical Theology*, bring these two terms into the following definition:

> Pastoral/practical theology is a place where religious belief, tradition and practice meets contemporary experiences, questions and actions and conducts a dialogue that is mutually enriching, intellectually critical, and practically transforming.[17]

As with Lyall in his discussion of pastoral care, Pattison and Woodward admit that the above definition 'suffers from all the problems that any definition does in trying to cope with a wide, open and developing sphere of activity'. And yet this summary is usefully general enough to cover the spreading remit of this most practical of theologies.

Historically, the term 'pastoral theology'[18] has been used primarily in the pastoral commitments of the Roman Catholic and Anglican Churches, whereas 'practical theology' is seen as a more scholarly and comprehensive term that covers situations and issues that include, and yet move beyond, the Church's pastoral encounters.[19] This broader remit is reflected in the decision of the British pastoral teachers' conference to rename itself in 1994 as the British and Irish Association of Practical Theology. This body produces an excellent journal, *Practical Theology*, which encourages research and comment in 'the development of pastoral studies and practical theology'.

In both fields these theologies have been seen traditionally as essentially about practical matters in church and parish. A manual dating from the early part of the twentieth century, which encouraged such pastoral practice, gave this advice in a chapter on 'work in the parish':

> There is another form of relaxation which is offered at times, and that is card-playing, either at a presbytery or at the house of some layman. In this there is no harm, but, as in other relaxations, moderation must be observed and company chosen. There may arise a temptation to give longer time than you honestly feel prudent to such amusement, that is, if this kind of thing appeals to you at all; and if you feel this, act honestly with yourself and limit the time you spend at it.[20]

Here the subversive dangers of relaxing with a parishioner are spelt out. Hopefully, practical and pastoral theologies have moved on since the 1930s!

Even so, this love affair with a workaday, pragmatic approach was fanned into further ardour by the advances of the new disciplines of dynamic psychology[21] and the psychology of religion[22] during the early years of the twentieth century. It is here that Edward Farley's criticism of much practical theology bears on the nature of pastoral theology too – a theology without the backbone of a substantial base of theory, 'a combination of a functionalist temper', focused on ministerial action,[23] and 'one or two extra theological disciplines that provide the scholarly aspect'.[24] This indictment has proved true both sides of the Atlantic, for many theological colleges and seminaries allowed pastoral theology, up to the 1980s, to be the Cinderella within the faculty, seeing its role as beyond the pale of academic theology and concerned solely with the messy business of human life, aided and abetted by theoretical input from such disciplines as psychology and sociology. I certainly found this to be case when I started part-time lecturing in pastoral studies at Trinity College in 1980, although I also gained increasing support from fellow lecturers in this enterprise during the following years.

And yet there is hope for a pastoral theology that is true praxis, where, as we have seen, there is a mutually transformative interplay between theory and practice. A wind of change blew into the clergy-dominated, pragmatic world of a psychologized pastoral care through the influence of Anton Boisen. His emphasis on a reflective theology that took seriously the hopes, loves and trials of 'living human documents' was later revived in Hiltner's shepherding perspective, which in turn sought a pastoral theology that 'draws conclusions of a theological order from reflection' on 'the operations and functions of the church and the minister'.[25] Such approaches have been further developed, modified or challenged by a range of contemporary theologians. Here there is a sharp awareness that, to quote Paul Ballard and John Pritchard, practical theology 'serves the life and work of the Christian community in its witness and service in and for the world . . . with its subject matter being the life and practice of the Church and the outworking of the gospel in every aspect of human community'.[26]

As we explore the five pathways to wholeness in the coming chapters, we will pick up the particular emphases brought by a number of today's practical and pastoral theologians. Throughout, we will be aware that each pathway tends to favour its own theological and spiritual stance. Although a great range of methodological positions can be taken up, broadly we will find two main polarities are returned to again and again: an emphasis on law, ethics, ground rules and foundational 'givens' on the one hand; and a stress on experience, story, imagination and personal and communal encounter on the other. Where too much weight is given to the first, there is a danger of steamrollering human need and diversity; where the second is overplayed, there may be a slippage into unbridled individualism and widespread relativism.

In my training in counselling and exploration of different methods I have met examples of both extremes. As we shall see in the next chapter, certain forms of biblical counselling are prone to a finger-wagging, confrontational approach that can browbeat the client, perhaps temporarily, into submission. At the other extreme, certain counselling styles that lean heavily on liberal, humanistic ideas can be so 'hands-off' and permissive that the client can easily lose his or her way.

In our search for a pastoral theological method we will seek to hold a balance between these approaches, open to an ethical foundation while at the same time being responsive to experience and story. The search is for a method that is both mindful of God-given universals and open to a liberational, gender-sensitive approach that values particularity and diversity.

A pastoral theological method

Pastoral theology in the early part of the twenty-first century is complex and still developing,[27] yet, I suggest, is marked by three strong features: an emphasis on case studies, the importance of hermeneutics, and a method that is essentially liberational.

Case studies

A wind of change blew into the clergy-dominated, pragmatic world of a psychologized pastoral care through the influence of Anton Boisen in the United States from the 1920s to the 1940s. Working as a hospital chaplain and yet brought low by his own episodic mental breakdowns, he pioneered a reflective theology that took seriously the social background and the hopes, loves and trials of patients, coining the term 'living human documents'. Mental illness, in this way of thinking, is seen as a fall into the dark places. And yet in spite of the sense of anguish and loss experienced, it may also prove to be a potential gateway to spiritual awakening, not least when the times of darkness and recovery are accompanied by supportive fellow travellers, be they friends, family members or trained psychiatric or pastoral carers.

The crucial component of Boisen's notion of 'living human documents' is the need to get the story right. Glenn Asquith sums up the importance of this for the busy pastor in a parochial setting. Here, as in all pastoral contexts, it is essential to find the time to learn 'the details and the background of the parishioner's situation' in order to be 'more effective' and, at the same time, 'to think theologically about human experience'.[28]

Stephanie, a young postgraduate in history, came to see me as a Christian who was struggling with her sexual identity and fearful of her lesbian tendencies. As an only child, she was overwhelmed by a dominant and controlling mother who seemed to rob her of a sense of 'being her own person' whenever she visited the parental home. Since her teen years, when she had 'crushes' on her female teachers, she had been drawn to a series of passionate relationships with women, either of her own age or slightly older – women whose self-lessness, social skills and humour she especially admired and coveted. Some chapters of the 'living human document' of her story were opened over the limited time I was able to see her, and because of her clear history of religious commitment our discussions included a focus on some elements of her thoughts and feelings about the links, if any, between her inner turmoil and her Christian faith. She declared a falling away from the happier former times of her discipleship and concluded that, although her mind could still see the relevance of Christianity, her emotional life did not match that conviction.

As in many clinical, counselling and pastoral encounters, here was an unresolved fragment of someone's 'living human document' that was shared over a limited period; yet, hopefully, it contained within its exposure to active listening and tentative interpretation the potential for transformative growth within a particular unfolding story of human experience and theological reflection.

Hermeneutics

Contemporary society has been described as a 'culture of interpretation,'[29] and as we have seen in the personal experience and pastoral work of Anton Boisen, theological reflection in pastoral care has been understood as getting the story right, with all the challenges of understanding, interpretation and application that entails.

Whereas the hermeneutics of the text, as in the interpretation of the Hebrew Bible and New Testament, is sharply focused on the original languages, the context and the minutiae of grammar, syntax and meaning, the hermeneutics of people's lives is in 'soft focus' as it seeks to understand story, motive and circumstance. This process, initiated by Boisen in the context of pastoral care, has been further explored in the United States by Charles V. Gerkin, a pastoral psychologist.

Gerkin, in the context of pastoral counselling, emphasizes the necessity for the pastoral carer to acknowledge his or her own **pre-understanding** as well as that of the person who is seeking help. We all need to have some idea of the presuppositions we bring to the pastoral encounter. For example, a pastoral counsellor who is aware of the difficult relationship she has with her mother may be wary of taking on a client who is an older woman; or someone considering spiritual direction may be daunted by his notion that a spiritual director is likely to be grim, stony-faced and over-critical rather than someone who offers to be a listening fellow pilgrim or soul-friend.

Further, the pastoral carer needs to be privy to the idea of the **hermeneutical circle,** a term first coined by Friedrich Schleiermacher in the early nineteenth century and used by most interpreters since. Gerkin sees this concept applying to the pastoral encounter in counselling in terms of a 'circular pattern that moves from the immediate counselling relationship to the arena of current life relationships, back to the counselling relationship itself'. This engagement is loosely structured by the twofold process of the counsellor's enquiry and the emergence of a range of 'interpretive possibilities'.[30] ·

Let me try to illustrate the importance of pre-understanding and the hermeneutical circle in a case study.

Grant, in his late thirties, married to Jane and with two children, phoned me to seek counselling. He had had a strong sense of God's calling to his present job – he was a solicitor – but after one year he was full of self-doubt and believed that he had misjudged that call. Jane had forfeited a fulfilling job as a teacher to make their move, and Grant's indecision was already threatening their marriage.

What pre-understandings did Grant and I bring to the early stages of the counselling relationship? He had shared a little of his story with the psychiatric friend of a colleague and had been advised to ask his GP for antidepressants. He resisted that step in that he wanted to 'understand' his conflict and, further, expected me to address the 'spiritual' as well as 'psychological' aspects of his situation. For my part, I was aware that I had mixed feelings about taking on this client. On the one hand, I was sympathetic with the view that, if possible, he should avoid medication, unless any resulting depression was deep enough to warrant drugs to lift his mood and facilitate the pastoral encounter. On the other hand, I felt reluctant to address his 'spiritual' needs, not from any desire to exclude the possibility of such exploration, but in order to avoid any compartmentalizing of this or that aspect of his life.

These pre-understandings were tacitly acknowledged and we entered into what proved to be an extended period of counselling. Within the developing relationship, Grant's story – his perceived call from God, his way of handling decisions that insufficiently engaged Jane's wishes, and the patterns built up in his life since childhood – was explored and tentatively interpreted. Although this softly focused approach centred on Grant's world, my own self-understanding was also illuminated and expanded by the pastoral encounter – not least in a fresh reminder how in my own life certain questionable decisions can be rationalized as 'God's will'.

Throughout this process the hermeneutical circle between us meant a frequent re-evaluation of how best to interpret Grant's life. At the end of many sessions, especially in the early months of counselling, I realized that my tentative conclusions about him might need reassessing and modifying as his story further unravelled. For example, one of my initial impressions of him was that he had a selfish preoccupation with his own destiny, at the expense of Jane, their children and other important figures in his life. In seeking to 'read' Grant as a 'living human document', his story 'spoke back' in ways that, after all, showed a deep desire for the best in the lives of those around him, albeit a desire that needed freeing from its blind spots. Eventually, a measure of mutual understanding between us began to nudge Grant forward into a widened and more accountable vision of the way ahead.

Liberation

The third dimension of our pastoral theological method is that of liberation, and this emphasis needs to be seen in the light of private and public inequities. The God of Israel and Jesus is a liberational God. As Moltmann puts it, 'Exodus theology is not yet resurrection theology, but resurrection theology must always include exodus theology and must again and again be embodied in acts that liberate the oppressed.'[31]

As is well known, a theology of liberation in modern times first emerged in Latin America in the 1960s, primarily in the Roman Catholic Church and in response to the gross injustices afflicting the poor and marginalized. Here was a theology that, to quote Stephen Pattison, was 'practical, contextual, and action-guiding',[32] deeply concerned with the social and political conditions that so powerfully suppressed the people.

In the 1980s and 1990s a handful of British pastoral theologians began to see that pastoral care, with its history of focusing on the individual and the psychological, desperately needed the perspectives of liberation theology to widen its horizons to embrace the social and political circumstances that could undermine people's sense of belonging and well-being.[33]

Elaine Graham's 'transformative Christian practice' is an instance of this bid to open up pastoral theology to the wider contextual issues of social and political injustice. She offers a profoundly liberationist method that is also open to feminist and narrative theologies. True to postmodernity's celebration of particularity and diversity, she puts forward a **practical wisdom** that is the very 'medium by which truth-claims and value-commitments come into existence'.[34] This formative wisdom serves to mould attitudes where human otherness is valued and where 'the irreducible difference and mystery of the other' demonstrates 'a moral community [that] is heterogeneous and pluralistic', rather than hidebound by 'a universal set of needs and qualities'.[35] Thus Graham, through the exploration of difference and otherness in the stories of women's experiences and the accounts of other marginalized groups, engages with the revelatory nature of practical wisdom.

To illustrate such disclosure, she cites a range of examples from the work of Nancy Fraser, in which a number of 'runaway' needs, starting as issues dealt with in the private domain and breaking loose into public consciousness, serve to reveal the mismatch between women's perceived needs and the established norms and meanings of a patriarchal society. Thus, self-help groups, tenants' associations and women's health groups have helped to redraw the boundaries between the 'public' and 'political' on the one hand, and the 'private' and 'domestic' on the other, on such issues as the valuing of housework, the need of childcare, accusations of 'date rape' and the realities of sexual harassment in the workplace.[36]

In July 2012 a report from the British Crime Survey[37] indicated that there could be as many as 1.2 million women and girls in the United Kingdom who are victims of domestic violence, and one in four women are likely to experience physical abuse at some point in their lifetime. Here, what is often jealously guarded as private needs to be brought into the open public gaze if there is to be the liberational effect of justice and a faithful level of pastoral care.

And so, Graham argues, the 'practical wisdom' of Christian practice needs to be guided by the question, 'What does it disclose/foreclose?'

In other words, we need to discover what values and preconceived ideas lie behind the pastoral encounter – both those that reveal what is just and liberating and those that expose what is unjust and restrictive. Graham acknowledges the tension between the traditions of history and contemporary experience, arguing that the latter, in, for example, the feminist movement, 'may reveal the foreclosures and fault-lines of historic practices'. Once more, we are reminded that we are set in a culture of interpretation, in which the past is not seen as 'a fixed and concrete event' so much as a source for disclosure, wherein 'the enduring availability of possible meanings' are 'available for reinterpretation'.[38]

In Graham's liberational method we see a pastoral theology that permeates a Christian practice that is gender-sensitive, charged with practical wisdom, respectful of otherness and seeking disclosure where appropriate. Here, the very difference of each pastoral engagement is allowed to speak forth its own reflectiveness and wise resolutions.

Thus, all in all we have a pastoral theological method that seeks a balance between its use of case studies, its 'hermeneutics of understanding' and its liberational style, providing, at its best, a God-centred praxis that can be described, simply, as 'doing theology'.

Doing theology: praxis revisited

In *Practical Theology in Action*, Paul Ballard and John Pritchard highlight the pastoral theological method of the 'pastoral cycle', in which **experience** is observed, leading to **exploration, reflection** and **action**, followed by further experience and the beginning of a fresh cycle.[39] This method mirrors the praxis of liberation theology, and one of the earliest examples of that theology in Britain is that of the pastoral commitment of Laurie Green, with his hands-on approach to 'doing theology'.

Based for ten years as vicar of the parish of Erdington, beneath Birmingham's Spaghetti Junction, and subsequently as principal of the Aston Training Scheme, which offered theological education to men and women prior to ordination training, Green has a great deal of first-hand experience of theological praxis in urban settings. In *Let's Do Theology*, he puts forward a 'new model' of theology that has arisen from the needs and situations of the people among whom he has worked, and pays particular attention to issues of 'liberation, context, action, power, oppression and spirituality'.[40] Here is an approach that may be used by individuals or groups and 'moves around continually from action to reflection and from reflection to action'.[41]

Green's earlier book, *Power to the Powerless*, provides rich illustration of this active and reflective theology. Soon after the founding in 1974 of the ecumenical project of St Chad's, Erdington, the combined Anglican and Methodist congregation carried out a major analysis of the locality and its needs, putting strong political pressure on local government to finance a community centre for the area.[42] This awareness was carried over in 1979 into the Parables in Action Group, a regular gathering of socially and racially mixed church members who, together with Laurie Green as their vicar, sought a 'democratized' theology, 'reclaimed as an essential component of every Christian's kitbag'.[43]

As the group looked at Gospel parables, its members began to appreciate two dynamic elements: Jesus' clear understanding of his contemporary reality, and his appreciation of the continuity between the Jewish people's history and the 'present and imminent reality of the Kingdom of Heaven'. Armed with these insights, they decided that, in order to find out how the parables really worked, they needed to be subject to a parabolic process themselves. And so, for the coming months, they resolved to use the identified ingredients of the parable to re-examine carefully the present realities in their part of Birmingham, research the history of its people and the structures within which they lived and, 'simultaneously and imaginatively', reflect on what God might want of them in the situation. Thus the group began to use the pastoral cycle as they searched the library archives, pored over maps and tape-recorded the memories of ageing residents to recover Erdington's past; in turn, they assessed 'present realities' through collecting demographic material, drawing up a checklist they could all use and sharing subjective impressions to balance objective data.

Newly aware that their locality was viewed as 'that area with lots of problems', the group raised a number of critical questions: What can be affirmed from our past? What from our past do we denounce? Which developments were good and which bad? Who made the decisions and whom did they affect? As they studied the contemporary scene they began to uncover a range of uncomfortable facts to which they had perhaps turned a blind eye, such as the degree of anxiety among residents concerning deteriorating properties, increasing street violence and high unemployment; the repeated reference in government reports to 'low moral and intellectual standards' and to 'problem families'; and the high level of air pollution recorded within their motorway-dominated skyscape.

Having identified the experience of powerlessness and frustration in the local community, the Parables in Action Group moved on to further reflection, realizing that their church had allowed itself to become distant from the people; most decisions on policy were made by outsiders, the present helping organizations were struggling and often ineffective, relevant skills and information were in short supply and the residents' low self-esteem was fed by popular myth and a biased media. Turning from a simple pragmatic approach that handled the Scriptures superficially, the group once more exposed themselves to the parables by acting out a few of them, to experience them 'from the inside'.

It was the story of the Good Samaritan, in particular, that revealed a range of stark correlations between the well-known parable and their situation. Amid the ensuing discussion, Madeleine, one of the group members, said, 'Just like the Samaritan, we are actually where the parishioners are, we're right on the spot. Even if we could only act as an information centre for people, that would be something.'[44] The group, seeking to keep its horizons wide as it reflected further, repeatedly came back to the notion of some sort of advice bureau, a need that had been pinpointed by a previous government survey, which stated that 87.6 per cent of the local residents had asked for just such a provision. After 14 months of deliberation and careful planning, supported by diocesan and other local money, the Community Advice Centre was opened in 1981, which it was hoped would be 'a small parabolic light in the present urban darkness'.

Looking back at the project, Sue, another group member, expressed the spirit of Green's democratized process of 'doing theology' well:

> We've been helped to discover that theology . . . can be done today. It's a practical exercise that involves action, like the setting up of an Advice Centre or whatever, and reflection upon that action. We have experienced a feeling of growing self-confidence in ourselves as theologians. Theology is too important to be left to the ministers of the Church.[45]

As we know, the problems addressed by Green and his community in the 1970s and 1980s are still with us today. Generally, the gap between the rich and the poor has widened and events such as the city riots of summer 2011 have revealed a groundswell of anger at society's perceived injustices. Louise Casey's report, *Listening to Troubled Families*, published in July 2012, highlighted:

- dysfunctional and unstable family structures;
- history repeating itself within families and between generations;
- extended family and antisocial networks within communities that reinforce destructive behaviour;
- the need for one assertive family worker who offers practical help and support but also sanction in dealing with families.[46]

And so we can readily see the need in contemporary society for those committed to a pastoral care that includes the social and political contexts of people's lives as well as the more personal and domestic aspects of their struggles.

Here we have established the value of a pastoral theological method that focuses on people's stories, their 'living human documents', their 'hermeneutics of life' and a liberational way forward, demonstrating its loving Christian praxis through 'doing theology' within a repeating interchange between experience, exploration, reflection and action. This will be our methodological basis as we unfold the mapping of the pathways to wholeness.

Mapping the pathways

A map-making enterprise, if it is to make sense to others, has to decide in advance what aspects of the terrain are to be surveyed and thus depicted. Is it to be a map that shows land use, sites of special scientific or conservational interest, the historical geography of an area, lines of communication, the morphology of the landscape or its underlying geology? Whatever the overall objective, there also have to be decisions about what is to be included and what excluded. So far, having taken our bearings within the territory of contemporary culture, we have begun to establish that our mapping of pathways to wholeness, in the context of Christian pastoral care, needs to include a portrayal of a pastoral theological method. And just as every cartographer – even a flat-earther! – has a view on the nature of what is being mapped, so we have worked towards a theology that is ably demonstrated in the praxis of Laurie Green's 'doing theology'.

Through the rest of this book we will consider five pathways to wholeness: biblical counselling, the healing ministries, pastoral counselling, spiritual direction and social transformation. As we explore these I will keep in mind the words of Robert Macfarlane in his book *The Old Ways: A Journey on Foot*:

> These are the consequences of the old ways with which I feel easiest: walking as enabling sight and thought rather than encouraging retreat and escape; paths as offering not only means of traversing space, but also ways of feeling, being and knowing.[47]

As we consider our pathways to wholeness let us see these routes through life not as escapes from reality but as 'enabling sight and thought' and helping us along ways that foster our 'feeling, being and knowing'.

In doing this I am not suggesting that these five pathways are the only routes through life, even though many of us will engage with one or more of these at some stage. For all of us, though, as we saw at the beginning of this chapter, there is a need for one-anotherness, the need to have someone else alongside at life's most difficult times. As Jim, in his late seventies and suffering from long-term cancer, said to his wife Amy on his admission to a local hospice in his final days: 'I can't die without you holding my hand.' It's a measure of the deeply committed pastoral care of the hospice movement that the sister arranged a private room for Jim with a second bed next to his for Amy. She lovingly held his hand, side by side, through the nights and then continued through the daylight hours over the next six days until his peaceful death. Here was the pathway to wholeness of everyday, practical care.

With regard to mapping the five pathways described in the following pages I propose to keep in mind seven aspects of each methodology:

- **focus**: that aspect of humanity focused on
- **hermeneutics**: the method of interpretation used
- **use of Scripture**: how and whether the Bible is used
- **metaphor**: the role adopted by the pastoral carer
- **spirituality**: the movement towards God adopted
- **theology**: the way God is thought about
- **keywords**: characteristic 'buzz words' of each pathway.

Table 1 may help the reader to have an overview of this proposed material.

Table 1 A map of pathways to wholeness

	BIBLICAL COUNSELLING	HEALING MINISTRIES	PASTORAL COUNSELLING	SPIRITUAL DIRECTION	SOCIAL CHANGE
FOCUS	Cognition Behaviour	Journey back	Relationships Psychological maturity	Inner journey Spiritual maturity	Community Environment
HERMENEUTICS	Exegetical	This-is-that	Soft-focus	Spiritual reading	Hermeneutics of suspicion
USE OF SCRIPTURE	Prescriptive	Therapeutic	Formative	Imaginative	Socio-political
METAPHOR	Teacher Guide	Healer Deliverer	Shepherd Pastor	Priest (desert-dweller, soul-friend, midwife)	Prophet Wise One
SPIRITUALITY	Evangelical Post-evangelical	Charismatic Pentecostal	Liberal Post-liberal	Catholic Eastern Orthodox Celtic	Liberational Feminist Intercultural
THEOLOGY	Propositional	Experiential	Correlational	Transcendental	Liberational
KEY WORDS	Word Cross	Spirit Power	Trinity Covenant	Presence Mystery	Exodus Freedom

As we engage with these five pathways, let us recall that the landscape is much more wondrous and complex than our attempts to map the possible ways through it. Maps are fun, but they are, inevitably, simplifications of the territory. Let the words of David Kelsey, writing of his own piece of descriptive cartography on the uses of Scripture, be an apt cautionary note at this stage of our journey:

> the work of God the Holy Spirit ... is not patient to systematic mapping ... Theological proposals are concerned with what God is now using scripture to do, and no degree of sophistication in theological methodology can hope to anticipate that![48]

2

Biblical counselling: the transformed mind

———————

Scripture ... is not an encyclopedia, but a tool for making encyclopedias. (Richard Lovelace)[1]

'Do you follow Jay Adams or Narramore?' This was the question I was accosted with by an earnest young man at the 1980 Christian Booksellers' Convention in London when my first book, *Restoring the Image*, was being launched. Were there really only two possible routes within the Christian counselling movement? With some relish, I replied, 'Neither!' Even so, this encounter set me thinking about the whole question of different methodologies in the vast field of counselling and psychotherapy, and in turn this led to my researching and writing the book *Roots and Shoots* over the next few years.

With the rise and rise of secular approaches to human need, a number of Christians had responded to Freud and his successors through the 1930s and beyond with **assimilation**, eagerly and uncritically absorbing such fetching new notions as that human malaise is, fundamentally, a question of neurosis rather than sin. In the 1940s and post-war years, the humanistic basis of Carl Rogers' psychology offered a non-directive, client-centred counselling style that became the central credo of the rapidly rising counselling movement. In many ways, this more optimistic and more relational method (human beings as persons) proved more readily enticing to Christian pastoral carers than the earlier blandishments of behaviourism (human beings as machines or simply higher animals) and of Freudian psychoanalysis (human beings as the sum of their instincts). In the face of such widespread assimilation of secular methodologies, a second response among Christians, that of **reaction**, began to find a voice, especially in the ranks of evangelicals from the 1960s onwards, many claiming to be even more 'biblical' than their Bible-loving predecessors. A third response by Christians, **dialogue**, has increasingly moved on to centre stage among those who were formerly assimilative or reactive, liberals and conservatives alike.[2] It is here that we come back to the young man's comments, since we can see in today's so-called 'biblical' counselling an evangelical spectrum, ranging from Jay Adams' more excluding and reactive style to Clyde Narramore's more integrational and potentially dialogical one.

On looking back at my own experience of counselling through the contexts of general practice, student health, theological college and church fellowship, I realize that I have comparatively rarely used the Bible in a direct and directional way. One of the few exceptions to this was during my encounters with Liz.

Liz came to see me with a history of anxiety and various compulsive behaviours that she felt mirrored those of her mother. In her early thirties, married for seven years and with two boys aged five and two, she also missed the security she had found in her father, who had died suddenly at the time of the birth of her first son. Although she spoke warmly of her father's 'ordinariness' and 'sense of humour', she admitted that she had never shed a tear over his death. For Liz, control meant everything, and since the birth of her children she had increasingly withdrawn from sex with her husband John, partly to avoid further pregnancy and partly from fear of the loss of being 'in charge'. She had become a Christian some years before and saw the importance of prayer and reading her Bible, but had long since stepped aside from these devotions. At the end of one of our counselling sessions, I gently suggested that, just for five minutes each day, she try to find time to read and reflect on a few verses from John 14—17. When I next saw her she said she'd had a better week, had started praying again and had turned to Psalm 23 to help her praise God for his care for her. She hadn't followed my suggestion of John's Gospel but, sensibly, had re-engaged with more familiar material.

Such experiences make me ask: What value does the Bible have in counselling? If it is to play its part, how is it to be used? Can the Bible be misused in counselling, and if so, how?

To help us explore the particular use of Scripture in 'biblical' counselling, let us consider its strengths and weaknesses in sections exploring exclusion, integration, the continuing debate, and finally, the way ahead.

Exclusion

David Powlison, in his monumental book *The Biblical Counseling Movement: History and Context*, sees Jay E. Adams as the founder of biblical counselling. Adams, an American Presbyterian strongly influenced by Dutch Calvinist philosophy, experienced a great deal of frustration during the early 1960s as he tried to counsel needy Christians with the Freudian and Rogerian insights of the day. He declares that his distinctive **nouthetic counselling** was launched in 1969 on the back of two cardinal influences: the behaviourism of O. Hobart Mowrer and the strongly held views on humanity of Cornelius Van Til, professor of apologetics at Westminster Theological Seminary in Philadelphia. Working under the tutelage of Mowrer in the summer of 1965, Adams readily responded to his mentor's open challenge to the widely accepted 'medical' model of mental illness and strong avowal of the 'moral' model, in which such terms as 'neurosis' and 'psychosis' are discarded in favour of an acknowledgement of real guilt and personal responsibility.[3] This re-evaluation of human 'mental' dysfunction in terms of sin rather than sickness was reinforced by Van Til's strong commitment to a 'two kingdoms' view of humanity, in which no one is neutral and all live out their lives in accordance with 'conceptions of reality' – either Christian or non-Christian. Van Til's conclusion is uncompromising: 'All men are either in covenant with Satan or in covenant with God.'[4]

Following these leads, nouthetic counselling incorporates the centrality of personal culpability, the universal dividing line between two kingdoms and, by inference, a strong suspicion towards 'secular' helping professionals such as clinical psychologists and psychiatrists.[5] In line with these emphases, Adams looks to *nouthesia* and *noutheteo* in the Greek New Testament as giving the context and flavour of Christian counselling methodology. These words, with their connotations of warning, instruction and admonition, are used in situations of relating within the Christian fellowship,[6] and in the Van Tilian sense are words of 'a world run by the counsel of God'.[7] Adams is consistent in his approach in that nouthetic counselling is committed to helping the *believer*, because, he writes, 'you can't *counsel* unbelievers in the biblical sense of the word (changing them, sanctifying them through the work of the Holy Spirit)':[8] conversion to Christ, he argues, is the prerequisite for authentic 'biblical change' through Christian counselling.

The biblical change that Adams writes of is, in essence, a change of mind and action that is effected through the open use of scriptural texts during counselling. This **cognitive behavioural** enterprise, in fact, sees the Bible's text as the resource for personal transformation: 'All that is needed to form values, beliefs, attitudes, and behavioral styles is in the Scriptures. Indeed, no other book can do so,' Adams says.[9] Further, Adams' methodology is largely **propositional** and **prescriptive** in its handling of the Bible; that is to say, biblical statements and propositions (the book of Proverbs and the Pauline epistles are happy hunting grounds)[10] are explicitly used within the counselling encounter and are often prescribed for the counsellee to learn and apply as 'homework' between sessions. The touchstone of Adams' approach is seen to lie in Paul's declaration to Timothy that 'All scripture is inspired by God and is useful for teaching, for reproof, for correction, and for training in righteousness' (2 Tim. 3.16), since, Adams states, this verse indicates that 'the Scriptures themselves are nouthetically oriented'.[11] Further, this biblical statement, and others of the same ilk, point to the reality that the nouthetic counsellor tends to be a **teacher** or highly directive **guide**.

Although Adams' methods have been much criticized for their confrontational and excluding style,[12] there is evidence that certain of his colleagues and followers, as is often the case where the legacy of a powerful leader is taken up by others, have adopted a less confrontational and more inclusive stance. In 1968 Adams was joined by John Bettler, a fellow pastor, in the founding of the Christian Counseling and Educational Foundation (CCEF) at Laverock in Pennsylvania. In 1976 the National Association of Nouthetic Counsellors was launched and its views began to be promoted through the *Journal of Pastoral Practice*. This organ, in turn, became the *Journal of Biblical Counseling* in 1993. Significantly, in an interview with Adams and Bettler that year, conducted by David Powlison, the narrower term 'nouthetic' counselling[13] had clearly given way to the more comprehensive one of 'biblical' counselling.[14] Further, Bettler's gentler and more inclusive approach is evident in the discussion between the three men. Where Adams' personal style is described as 'tough' and at times 'overwhelming', Bettler says of himself, 'If you aren't an exuberant person, counseling won't work if you start shouting'; where Adams focuses on training the ordained as counsellors, Bettler widens the remit to include lay people; and where Adams follows Van Til closely in emphasizing 'the antithesis between belief and unbelief', Bettler seeks, less confrontationally, to 'recycle' error 'in the light of truth'.[15]

And yet, given the commitment of a nouthetic counselling that has claimed the high ground of biblical counselling, there remains the need to clarify a stance that is, given its pedigree as a reaction to a psychologized culture, essentially **excluding**. John Bettler, arguing from a Presbyterian tradition that looks back to the Westminster Confession of 1646, seeks to begin the process of establishing a 'confession of faith for those who claim to be biblical counselors'. Acknowledging the differences among such, he goes on to say that 'we have stronger commonalities', including a Trinitarian creed, which also, in accord with evangelical orthodoxy, declares a belief in 'the authority of the Word of God' and that the Bible is 'the infallible rule of faith and life inspired of God'. In the context of applying such a standpoint to the counsellor's view on the place of the past in the counsellee's life, he declares the need 'to do the dangerous job of drawing circles, drawing lines', where anyone 'within the circle is biblical', anyone 'outside the circle is not'.[16]

David Powlison, who describes himself as a 'sympathetic critic' of Adams' approach, points to the origins of nouthetic counselling in 1965, its popularity in the 1970s, its comparative decline in the 1980s and its resurgence from the 1990s onwards. In May 1982, at a time when Adams' counselling methods were being hotly debated in the United Kingdom, three of us, David J. Atkinson, Richard D. Winter and myself, arranged to meet him at Hildenborough Hall, Kent, to discuss his methodology. At a personal level we found him friendly and good-humoured, although his stance against psychiatry, psychotherapy and all secular influence was clear and uncompromising.

Powlison summarizes Adams' excluding approach in these words:

> In his treatment of psychology, Adams is best understood as a rhetorician. His intentions were partisan, with no pretense of scholarly dispassion. He wrote polemically, to persuade groups of people to act: to inform, to convince, to motivate hearers to do something about what he proclaimed.[17]

Integration

Where Adams' excluding approach is like a journey in a city tram, a journey that is tightly defined within its tramlines, the integrational approaches to biblical counselling are more like travelling by car or bike, where there are no rigid restrictions that prevent an exploration of routes through the wider landscape.

In the United States

During the decade in which Jay Adams began to struggle with his perceived nemesis of the secular psychologies and psychotherapies, an alternative approach to biblical counselling, that of integration between psychology and theology, gained an increasingly strong foothold in North America.

The first glimmer of a bridging between the psychological and theological in evangelical circles began to show in 1952 with the founding of the Christian Association for Psychological Studies (CAPS) around a small nexus of Reformed psychiatrists and psychologists. In the late 1950s Clyde Narramore was in the vanguard of more populist conservative Christian speakers who were also trained in psychology. 1965 saw the founding of the Graduate School of Psychology at Fuller Theological Seminary, whose aim was 'to "integrate" conservative Protestant faith with modern psychology's insights and therapies'.[18] This catchword of 'integration', in an evangelical theological and psychological context, is defined by David Powlison:

> Though the definition of 'integration' was much controverted, its common denominator could be found in the emergence of a new kind of professional, new both in ecclesiastical and mental health circles: a conservative Protestant psychotherapist who intended to take both halves of that designation with equal seriousness.[19]

While Adams wrote and lectured through the initial heyday of nouthetic counselling in the 1970s, his rivals and critics in the integrational movement became increasingly established through the founding of their institutions and learned journals. At times, the estrangement between these two groups was like that of two dark fish swimming in ink.

In 1969 Gary Collins, a leading integrationist, was appointed as Trinity Evangelical Divinity School's first professor of pastoral psychology. A year later Bruce Narramore, a clinical psychologist and Clyde Narramore's nephew, became the founding dean of the Rosemead Graduate School of Professional Psychology, and in 1973 he began to edit the newly formed *Journal of Psychology and Theology*, committed to 'serve as a forum for the integration and application of psychological and biblical information'. This decade also saw the proliferation of books from the emerging stable of evangelical psychologists and psychotherapists, including Gary Collins' *The Rebuilding of Psychology: An Integration of Psychology and Christianity* (1977) and John D. Carter and Bruce Narramore's *The Integration of Psychology and Theology: An Introduction* (1979).

While the heavy criticisms of Jay Adams' more fundamentalist and excluding style of biblical counselling increased in the late 1970s and 1980s, the rise of the integrational 'evangelical psychotherapists' continued unabated during this period. In 1982 the second learned journal of the integration movement, the *Journal of Psychology and Christianity*, was launched to 'provide scholarly interchange among Christian professionals in the psychological and pastoral professions'. In 1985, Kirk E. Farnsworth's *Wholehearted Integration: Harmonizing Psychology and Christianity Through Word and Deed* was a fresh landmark in the popularizing and professionalizing of the integrational biblical counselling movement.

Even so, there were some influential voices who seemed caught between Adams' unashamed biblicism and the integrationists' more expansive methodologies. Outstanding among these is Larry Crabb, who trained as a clinical psychologist and worked as a counsellor in a university setting and private practice through the 1970s. His books *Basic Principles of Biblical Counseling* (1975) and *Effective Biblical Counseling* (1977) have been widely influential on both sides of the Atlantic.

Although supportive of Jay Adams in nouthetic counselling's early years, Crabb developed a cautiously integrational style, seeking to put forward 'a solidly biblical approach to counselling' which 'draws from secular psychology without betraying its Scriptural premise' and maintains belief in 'an inerrant Bible and an all-sufficient Christ'.[20]

In the United Kingdom

It has become a truism that innovations in North America have often stirred new beginnings in Britain a decade later. With the rapid advance of information technology in recent years, though, that transatlantic influence has speeded up. Along with the eastward flow since the Second World War of nylons, chewing gum, blue jeans, country and western music, 'shoulder to shoulder' politics and Apple Macs, American biblical counselling approaches have also been exported to our shores. However, the picture is a mixed one, with some home-grown elements establishing fresh ideas for Christian counselling and other participants, especially among evangelicals, looking to the United States and its biblical counselling methods.

While working as a Reader in an Anglican parish in the 1960s, I vividly remember the stir of interest among clergy at the founding of the Clinical Theology Association (CTA), under the aegis of Frank Lake, in 1962. Here, quite suddenly it seemed, was an attempt, on British soil, to bring together theological and psychological thinking. This organization, with its headquarters at Lingdale, Nottingham, sought to train a network of clinical tutors to dissem-inate further training in human relations, pastoral care and coun-selling. Known as the Bridge Pastoral Foundation since Lake's death in 1982, CTA's fundamental remit was an integrational one, seeking to 'promote an understanding between the disciplines of psychiatry and theology'.

Selwyn Hughes, a Pentecostalist pastor who, through an emotional breakdown in 1958, became increasingly committed to the world of pastoral care and counselling, looked to the biblical approaches of Clyde and Bruce Narramore and, most influentially, to the work of Larry Crabb. His early commitment to revival initiated the Crusade for World Revival (CWR) in 1965, but in 1975 his prime interest turned towards biblical counselling, and he and his colleague Trevor Partridge initiated a 'teaching and training ministry' that became incorporated into the Institute of Christian Counselling. Like Crabb, Hughes established a 'cautiously integrational' approach, blending a strong belief in the Bible's inerrancy with carefully selected perspec-tives from secular psychology. In 1998 a partnership was developed between CWR and the London School of Theology, in which a joint honours degree course in Theology and Counselling was developed, combining a biblical theology with, for example, cognitive behav-ioural theory and practice.

The early 1980s saw the emergence of a number of para-church Christian counselling organizations in the UK, including Care and Counsel in London, Network Counselling and Training in Bristol and the Oxford Christian Institute for Counselling in Oxford. The range of such bodies multiplied throughout the country during the 1980s and 1990s, espousing a number of methodologies along a spectrum from the more excluding forms of biblical counselling through to a range of integrative styles.

In the early days of some of these institutions, the battle between exclusion and integration being fought in the United States was mirrored in the UK. For example, my own involvement in the initial formation of Network in Bristol saw a struggle, albeit a courteous one, between the 'Bible only' approach of Jim Craddock of Scope Ministries (seeking a British satellite from its home base in Oklahoma City) and my own integrational methodology. The latter won the day and a training programme was set up, seeking to integrate a Bible-based theology with a stress on the therapeutic relationship and a careful appraisal of a range of secular methodologies. As with many other Christian counselling services, Network has developed into a highly professionalized body, with accreditation from the British Association for Counselling and Psychotherapy.

The integrative approach continued into the late 1980s and 1990s with the setting up of the Network of Christians in Psychology (NeCIP) in 1989, as a forum for the integration of faith with psychological training and experience, and the launch of the Association for Christian Counsellors (ACC) in 1992. In the latter, I and others were involved with a similar interchange to that experienced a decade earlier at Network. I vividly remember our steering committee meetings when John Turner, Network's second director, and I battled with the other members over the precise wording of ACC's Statement of Faith and definition of Christian counselling. John and I espoused a relatively integrative viewpoint and sought a wider, inclusive remit for ACC than the more excluding stream of the British Association of Biblical Counsellors (ABC), set up in 1984.[21] The outcome was an admixture of ABC's influence and that of a number of more integrational counselling organizations to form a monitoring and accrediting body for Christian counsellors, supervisors and training courses. This association has gone from strength to strength, from its early days striving to move beyond too narrow a definition of Christian counselling, under the chairmanship of Mervyn Suffield, to a truly integrational body under, among others, Julia Muir, David Depledge and Greta Randle, with the initiation of a Pastoral Care Foundation Course in 2010.[22]

The continuing debate

Evangelicalism has a long history of fragmentation and infighting. And this tendency to partisanship often hinges on its desire to be faithful to Scripture on the one hand, and on the other on its understanding of and wrestling with biblical interpretation. Talking with a married couple in their late sixties over a cup of tea recently, my wife Joy and I were taken aback freshly by the seeming rigidity of their conservative evangelicalism. They had recently moved from a more charismatically inclined church on the understandable grounds that, they felt, God's Word was not being adequately heeded by the leadership. At times they seemed to elevate the Bible and its perceived inerrancy as a faultless lodestone, a monolith of utterance that brooked no debate.

We have already seen something of the polarization, initially in the United States and later in the United Kingdom, between an excluding, 'Bible-only' approach and an integrative style that seeks to blend scriptural and psychological insight. We have noted the decline of the former in the 1980s and the rise of the latter during the same decade. The 1990s began to see a reversal of this state of affairs, with a more conservative trend emerging among the evangelical psychotherapists and some heavy criticism from positions even further to the 'right' than Jay Adams' methodology.

In 1992 Gary Collins, one of the leading and most popular integrationists, was invited to revitalize the languishing American Association of Christian Counselors (AACC). Collins and other conservative evangelicals had begun to criticize the well-established Christian Association of Psychological Studies (CAPS), seeing this organization as being enticed by a more liberal agenda. Under Collins' influence, the AACC held strongly to a traditional biblical theology, viewing counselling as essentially a Christian ministry and bringing out a third integrational journal, *The Christian Counselor*, as a populist and practical rival to its more academic counterparts and avowedly conservative evangelical in its remit. AACC rapidly developed a strong following, with close on 50,000 members by 2012.

We have already seen the mounting criticisms of Jay Adams' nouthetic counselling during the 1980s. For John Bettler, Adams' close colleague in the 1960s, there was an increased parting of the ways. Bettler found that Adams' style of counselling tended to misuse the Bible, was concerned with external behaviour rather than the inner workings of the human mind and emotions, was neglectful of social context, overly directive and unfair to the true views of psychologists.[23]

Although most of the reaction against Adams' excluding style came from the integrationists, surprise attacks in both North America and Britain have come from even stricter 'Bible-only' stables.

Martin Bobgan, an educational psychologist, and his wife Deirdre, pioneered an excluding approach to Christian counselling in the 1970s. Their 'spiritual' counselling sought to filter out psychotherapeutic ideologies that are seen to contradict Scripture, arguing that 'all nonorganically related mental-emotional disorders have a spiritual, Christ-centred solution rather than a psychological, self-centred solution'.[24] However, in 1995 they openly repented of their previous support of Jay Adams and the biblical counselling movement.[25] They not only dismissed all biblical counselling that sifted the secular psychologies, however carefully, they also roundly condemned the more cautiously integrational styles of Gary Collins, John Bettler and Larry Crabb. Rejecting the very notion of counselling within the life of the Church, they thereby dismiss all probing of a person's psychological make-up and training in counselling skills:

> What some who counsel may not realize is that it is entirely unnecessary to use a manual or even to discuss the problem that led the person to seek counsel. Counsel using the Scripture and empowered by the Holy Spirit is effective whether or not one even discusses the [presenting] problem. This is probably the most difficult idea to communicate to those who are dependent on a manual, method, or training program. A believer empowered by the Holy Spirit and armed with Scripture never has and never will need a manual, method or training program![26]

A similar voice to the Bobgans' in the UK is that of E. S. Williams, a public health medical doctor who has written a great deal of material that is highly critical of a psychological approach to human need, arguing a strong excluding 'Bible-only' position.

In his *The Dark Side of Christian Counselling*, no one in the realms of psychiatry, psychotherapy, psychology and counselling is spared: Freud, Adler, Maslow, Rogers and Ellis[27] are dismissed as 'secular humanists who, in their lives and theories, rejected the God of

Scripture';[28] the question that an integrational approach in Christian counselling might be 'introducing dangerous false teaching into the church' is raised;[29] and cautiously integrational biblical counsellors like Larry Crabb[30] and Selwyn Hughes[31] are also found wanting. Having examined the assumptions and methods of a range of Christian counsellors, he concludes:

> From the evidence that we have uncovered, there can be no doubt that such Christian counselling is not a legitimate part of Christian ministry but an imposter that is misleading the church. We have come face to face with false teaching that has slipped into the church. We are led to the inevitable conclusion that the Christian counselling movement, which is propagating false teaching, poses a serious threat to the church and the Gospel.[32]

The way ahead

Who can see the way ahead in any human story, let alone that of the biblical counselling movement? We have seen, in turn, its rise, decline, outright rejection and recent renewal. What lessons, if any, can we take from this story? I would like to suggest two areas for consideration: the use of the Bible, and a new spirituality.

The use of the Bible

In recent years I have engaged with online debates at Fulcrum, an 'open' evangelical body committed to 'renewing the evangelical centre'. The level of contributions varies greatly, but the organizers are very generous in allowing a wide range of opinions to be expressed. Even so, I and others have often been accused of being 'liberal' or 'revisionist' when we have sought to debate certain interpretations of Scripture. I have no problem with being labelled this way, but the reaction sometimes met in our discussions points to a strong commitment to the surface meaning of a text, at times regardless of context and cultural background.

Alister McGrath traces this emphasis on the self-evident nature of Scripture, which we find in at least some biblical counselling, to the primacy of reason inherited from the renewal of evangelical faith during the eighteenth century.[33] He shows how this rationality permeated conservative Calvinistic theology in North America, including the biblical theology of Charles Hodge and Benjamin Breckinridge Warfield in the nineteenth century. For Hodge, McGrath writes: 'words can be known directly and immediately by the human mind, without the need for any intermediaries. To know the words of Scripture is thus to know immediately the realities to which they relate.'[34]

Further, what is the essential difference between the excluding and the integrational biblical counsellor in their use of the Bible? We have seen hints of this distinction in our survey of the biblical counselling movement, and the various details of the disagreements between the two trends can be summed up in two words: **God's revelation.**

The 'Bible-only' counsellor stresses **special revelation** to the neglect of general revelation. In other words, the excluding biblical counsellor focuses on the scriptural text in terms of specific times, places, people and propositions. Here there is supreme emphasis on what are seen as the 'givens' of creation, humanity's fall from grace, redemption in Christ, the coming of the Holy Spirit and the 'last things'. Special revelation is remedial in that 'it is God's means of reaching the *sinner* with saving, restorative truth'.[35] Without disputing the vital importance of this understanding of the Bible, there is the danger of reducing Scripture to 'a code book of theological ordinances',[36] in the sense seen in the quotation that heads this chapter where Richard Lovelace declares that the Bible 'is not an encyclopedia'. It is not a manual; it is not a reference book; it is not simply a 'how to do it' handbook. Where the Bible is seen as a rule-book, God's rich and wondrous world is perceived, in essence, as 'enemy territory'. So, for example, the discipline of psychology is firmly put in its place. It is allowed to be 'illustrative' and 'provocative'[37] but is not permitted to enter into face-to-face dialogue with theology, let alone contemplate an integration of its insights and perspectives with the latter discipline.

In contrast, the integrational biblical counsellor has sought to be open to **general revelation** as well as special revelation. Here is a common-grace theology which sees that the Bible also points out into God's world. As Berkouwer puts it, writing in the Calvinist tradition, God's general revelation sees 'the sovereign working of God in nature, in history, and in human existence'.[38] This perspective is evident in the Hebrew Bible: for example, in 'nature psalms' such as

Psalm 19, 'The heavens are telling the glory of God; and the firmament proclaims his handiwork'; in God's galaxy of created wonders in Job 38—41, where God assails Job with relentless questions, asking, 'Where were you when I laid the foundation of the earth?'; and in the beautiful lyric of Proverbs 8, where God's companionate Wisdom declares her joy in being daily Yahweh's 'delight, rejoicing before him always, rejoicing in his inhabited world and delighting in the human race' (8.30–31). Similarly, in the New Testament, we see the thread of general revelation in John's Prologue: 'What has come into being in him was life, and the life was the light of all people' (1.3–4); Romans 2.15 points to the presence of God's law as 'written on' the hearts of unbelieving Gentiles; and the great Christological first chapter of Colossians shows that within the created order, 'in him all things hold together' (1.17).

With Lovelace, integrative biblical counsellors view the Bible as 'a tool for making encyclopedias' in that they see a scriptural mandate to explore and reflect on all that God's world has to offer. With this perspective on Scripture, integrative biblical counsellors have often cited the maxim 'all truth is God's truth', quoting the philosopher Arthur Holmes on the basis of his Christ-centred biblical theology. Thus, integration is sought between theological truth and psychological truth, on the grounds that God 'is the eternal and all-wise creator of all things' and 'his creative wisdom is the source and norm of all truth about everything'.[39]

In each of the pathways we look at in this book there is a distinctive way in which the place of Scripture is evident. In this first pathway, biblical counselling, we have seen a strong factionalism between the 'Bible-only' approach of the excluding styles and the more open-handed use of Scripture among the integrationists. In the former there may be a large, black-covered Bible (usually the King James Version!) sitting menacingly at hand as the biblical counsellor (usually a man, at least in the early years of the movement) invites the client in to begin the session. In the latter, the integrationist counsellor is likely to be equally knowledgeable of Scripture but will keep that knowledge at the back of his or her mind, sensitive to there being a right time and place to raise such things, if at all, in any particular counselling encounter.

Kate was in her early thirties when she came to see me. She had come reluctantly, persuaded by a friend to do so, and was seeking help for feelings of inadequacy and self-dislike. Over the coming weeks she became more relaxed, smiled less automatically and, at times, came close to tears.

Her father was an authoritarian figure who strongly favoured Kate's older sister, Sonia, who had excelled at sport and music at school, achieved well at university, had married a gifted lawyer and produced two beautiful children. Although Kate's mother tried to compensate for her father's favouritism towards Sonia, Kate still felt deeply undermined by his comments: 'Why can't you take a leaf out of your sister's book?' 'You know what you are? You're pathetic!' And worst of all, 'I sometimes wonder where you came from!'

From her teen years onwards, Kate had learned to cope by presenting a smiling exterior and was seen as dependable in her various secretarial jobs. Even so, she seemed aloof and was especially wary of male company. She treated younger men with suspicion and older men with fear. Through a friend's prayers she tentatively committed her life to Christ, although the church they both attended never seemed to penetrate her defensive manner.

During counselling, her true feelings began to surface. Here was a deep anger towards her undermining father and the God who had dealt her such a poor emotional and developmental hand. As we talked about her negative feelings and the sense of guilt they aroused, it occurred to me to say, 'Do you know, Kate, God wants you to be angry with him!' I had recently been reflecting on the Psalms of Lament, in which the psalmist expresses his complaints to God vehemently. I pointed out to Kate that although most of the Psalms of Lament close with some reassurance or vow to praise, one of them, Psalm 88, concludes with these bleak words:

> Your wrath has swept over me; your dread assaults destroy me. They surround me like a flood all day long; from all sides they close in on me. You have caused friend and neighbour to shun me; my companions are in darkness.

Although these verses, on the face of it, seemed to offer Kate little comfort, it turned out that they resonated well with her situation. She needed to find permission, like the psalmist, to be angry with God, to tell him how she felt, to ask for forgiveness and to find strength to forgive her father. Within this process, she was also helped by the fresh awareness that Christ himself had faced an even worse dereliction on the cross when he cried, 'My God, my God, why have you forsaken me?'

This example is not given as a template for so-called biblical counselling. It points rather to the sensitivity and flexibility needed if Scripture, at any stage, is going to be used openly in counselling. It would be salutary for those who seek to use a Bible in counselling to imagine it having a large warning notice on its cover: 'THIS BOOK IS DANGEROUS. HANDLE WITH CARE!' Gary Sweeten, an American counsellor I met in the 1980s, said that the Bible may be the 'sword of the Spirit', but we are not to wield it, to 'perform open heart surgery' at every turn – a heavy-handed approach to people in need that 'exudes death'.

A new spirituality

We have traced the story of biblical counselling from the post-war years through to the beginning of the twenty-first century. Over the same period there have been marked changes within evangelicalism, the nurturing mother of all 'biblical' counselling. Robert E. Webber charts this development in *The Younger Evangelicals*:

- traditional evangelicals (1950–1975): a modern world-view
- pragmatic evangelicals (1975–2000): a transitional world-view
- younger evangelicals (2000–): a postmodern world-view.

There is, of course, considerable overlap between these three groups. For example, the 'traditional evangelical' is still very much alive and well. Here there is a strong commitment to the rational, and the propositional statements of Scripture are prioritized. We have seen this trend in the 'Bible-only' branches of biblical counselling, where the 'hard facts' of science are valued but the more diffuse world of psychology, sociology and the arts are treated with suspicion. In his partially integrational approach, Selwyn Hughes holds to the best of traditional evangelicalism in *Christ Empowered Living*, a book full of Christ-centred advice to find stability 'in an unstable world'.

I distinctly remember the emergence of the 'pragmatic evangelical' in the 1970s in Bristol. Since the late 1960s, when a friend bought me a copy of Francis Schaeffer's *Escape from Reason* (1968), I had continued in the modernist frame of mind of the traditional evangelical and yet was beginning to apply that rationality to the complex world of the arts and specific cultures. A group of us set up the Bristol Christian

Arts Group, affiliated to the Arts Centre Group in London. We met regularly to engage earnestly with such diversity as the meaning of the lyrics in Leonard Cohen's songs, the aesthetics of landscape gardening, the intricacies of Dooyeweerd's philosophy and the sheer delight of listening to late medieval music played on a bass viol.

This was also the period of 'therapeutic culture' within Christianity, and we have seen the evangelical aspect of this in the more integrational trend in biblical counselling. At the same time there was a plethora of pragmatic 'how-to' books being written by evangelical psychologists and psychotherapists, such as James Dobson's *Dare to Discipline* (1970) and Larry Crabb's *The Marriage Builder* (1982).

Robert Webber defines the 'younger evangelicals', a term that emerged at the dawn of the twenty-first century, as a group that includes not only those who are 'young in age' but also those who are 'young in spirit', and part of 'a movement they represent as a new or young movement'.[40] Here we have those within evangelicalism who embrace the best of postmodernism.[41] This development is characterized by, for example:

- an understanding 'of the heart' as well as the head;
- a valuing of story – personal, communal and biblical;
- a rediscovery of symbol and ritual in worship;
- a sense of being at home in the world of the internet and electronic communication;
- a fostering of intergenerational and intercultural relationships;
- a special commitment to the needs of the poor;
- a celebration of the arts, creativity and imagination.

Here there is no compromise of foundational Christian faith. In fact, many younger evangelicals hold strongly to biblical absolutes. As Webber puts it, 'The clash between twentieth- and twenty-first-century evangelicals is not over truth but over the cultural garb in which truth is clothed.'[42]

Alongside Webber's contribution to this debate in post-9/11 America, there have been a number of British writers who have voiced similar observations of a newly shaped evangelicalism. Questions are being asked of the world of the traditional evangelical, and fresh horizons are opened up. British contributors include Nigel Wright in *The Radical Evangelical* (1996), Alistair Ross in *Evangelicals in Exile* (1997), and Dave Tomlinson in the hotly debated *The Post-Evangelical*

(1995) and in his 'progressive orthodoxy' found in *Re-Enchanting Christianity* (2008). For Tomlinson, 'a consciousness of truth is ... found less in propositional statements and moral certitudes and more in symbols, ambiguities and situational judgements'.[43] Another increasingly popular example of these postmodern trends in evangelicalism and other branches of Christianity can be seen in the flourishing of the annual Greenbelt Festival, founded in 1974, in which the arts, expressions of faith and issues of justice are explored.

The world of biblical counselling also reflects this paradigm shift between the rationalizing certainties of its earlier years through to the wider horizons of the twenty-first century. Gary Collins, in the third edition of his book *Christian Counseling* (2007), describes the spirituality of a 'new Christian counselling', in which the counsellor is interactive with the person being helped, and is likely to show some vulnerability, be culturally aware and be conscious of the empowering by the Holy Spirit. In a similar vein, Larry Crabb describes the development in 2002 of his New Way Ministries in *The Pressure's Off* (2012); without refuting his foundational work in biblical counselling, he explores the value of the healing ministries and spiritual direction – pathways to wholeness that will be discussed in Chapters 3 and 5 respectively.

And so, in the years following my conversation with the young man in 1980, described at the beginning of this chapter, I now have a clearer picture of where I stand with regard to the only two options offered me: 'Do you follow Jay Adams or Narramore?' My own approach has sought an integrational methodology, initially comparable to Narramore's style, but since the early 1980s increasingly open to the rich material offered by our four other pathways.

In our next chapter we will begin an exploration of the second of these: the healing ministries.

3

Healing ministries: the forward gain

————— ◆•◆•◆ —————

'The wound is healed,' he said, 'I am whole, I am free.' Then he
bent over and hid his face in his arms, weeping like a boy.
(Ursula Le Guin)[1]

The year was 1979, the place was Christ Church vicarage, Clifton,
Bristol, and the situation was several weeks into my second period
of blindness – with, it seemed at that stage, no prospect of medical
or surgical cure. At the recommendation of a friend, Joy and I were
meeting with a visiting healer from the Midlands, a woman in her
early thirties or thereabouts, a leading member of a house church
who was said to have been instrumental in many dramatic experiences of healing. We had mixed feelings about the extravagant claims
of her street credibility; yet after a first bout of blindness that lasted
eight months, followed by a few one-eyed, sighted months, and now,
after a holiday on Colonsay, a return to physical darkness, we also
reckoned that there was nothing to lose in continuing to look to God
for reprieve through his servants' ministries.

The experience was not a happy one. There were five of us present:
Gloria, the healer, two younger women (our mutual friend and one
who worked with Gloria), Joy and myself. We sat in a semi-circle
about the hearth of an upstairs room and discussed my condition –
the diabetes, the consequent blindness and the undulating symptoms
of brucellosis. All seemed hopeful until Gloria asked whether I had
been 'baptized in the Spirit'. My understanding of Scripture was
such that I believed that a Trinitarian God cannot be divided up;
thus, having opened my life to Jesus the Spirit-Baptizer, I replied
in the affirmative. However, this response did not fit with Gloria's
'second blessing' theology and her view that healing is closely linked
to 'receiving the Spirit'. A further setback in this supposedly therapeutic encounter came a little later when, in reply to another leading

question, I had to declare that I could not be *sure* that God would heal me miraculously, either immediately or gradually, this side of heaven. Gloria was clearly unhappy with this apparent lack of faith. In reply to my references to the stories of Job and St Paul's 'thorn in the flesh', she took the little remaining wind out of my expectant sails by saying, 'You can only claim Job's experience if you are as good as he was; you can only identify with Paul's situation if you have had the sort of visions of God that he had.'

What more could be said? We had reached a theological and pastoral impasse. And yet, wisely, we set the theorizing aside, and Gloria laid her hands on my bowed head and prayed vehemently for my healing. Echoing her prayers in our hearts, Joy and I made our way out into the winter streets of Clifton. Two months later I had a second major operation on my recalcitrant right eye and the clearing of sight began once more. That unilateral vision, with the exception of the need for cataract surgery in 1990, has held well since; the brucellosis continued to debilitate over the following 18 years or so, although its grip has completely vanished in the last few years.

Clebsch and Jaekle, in evaluating the history of pastoral care, have written that the function of healing, compared with guiding, sustaining and reconciling, is, in the context of the last 40 years of the twentieth century, both the 'most problematical' and the 'most open to new and fresh expression'.[2] In many ways my encounter with Gloria highlights both what is 'problematical' and what makes for hopeful change in Christian healing, raising innumerable questions – pastorally, experientially and theologically. Were we wise to engage with her in the first place? What exactly did we expect of her? Of our friend? Of God? Did our clash of biblical hermeneutics matter in terms of expectant faith and prayer? Was Gloria, after all, instrumental in some way in my improvement of sight, or was its restoration entirely due to the God who can heal through a surgeon's hands? And what of the brucellosis? Is a delay of 18 years for answered prayer stretching the limits of credulity? What is healing anyway? Is peace of mind and heart through the trials of surgical intervention and chronically recurring illness not worth as much, or more, than a physical restoration that may work against life's learning curve?

It is questions like these, arising from the praxis of the so-called 'healing ministries', that we need to consider in this chapter as we examine our second pathway to wholeness.[3] The subject is a big one and is fraught, as we have seen in our brief example, with a range of theoretical and practical issues that weave in and out of what may be called a theology of healing and a theology of suffering or, alternatively, a theology of power and a theology of weakness.

And so, keeping in mind these two aspects of the healing ministries, we will address the place of healing and sustaining in the story of the Church, followed by the more controversial areas of inner healing and deliverance, before exploring the way ahead for healing within the reality of human suffering.

The Church and healing

One might say that from the 1960s onwards sections of the Christian Church, especially those influenced by the successive waves of the charismatic movement, John Wimber's 'power healing', the 'Toronto blessing' and, most recently, Neil Anderson's emphasis on 'Freedom in Christ' and the 'New Wine ministries', have developed an almost unhealthy preoccupation with health. And yet behind this surge of interest lies a long history of pastoral care in which the Church's call to heal in the name of Christ has waxed and waned through intermittent periods of scepticism and expectancy. Perhaps the most important thing for Christian healing ministries in today's culture is to steer a trusting (but not naive) and hope-giving route between the rigorous scientism of modernity, where even the possibility of divine intervention is derisible, and the easy-believism of postmodern plurality with its often tenuously held boundaries between meaning and magic.

Health and healing

Before giving a brief overview of some of the salient features of the healing function throughout the history of pastoral care, it is worth clarifying something of what is meant by health and healing.

The word 'health' comes from the same Old English stock that gives us 'hale' (as in 'hale and hearty') in the northern dialect and 'whole' in the Midlands and southern parts of England. Although the word is commonly used today as a synonym of 'fitness', in the sense of 'soundness of body', its original meaning was much more closely linked with the concept of well-being in every aspect of human life. This comprehensiveness accords well with the Judaeo-Christian tradition, as is brought out by Morris Maddocks when he writes: 'Health can never be equated with human wellness and an absence of disease. Health is to do with the totality of creation, with the Creator himself.'[4]

With respect to 'healing', Clebsch and Jaekle declare, in a similar vein to Maddocks, that 'healing is more than mere restoration, for it includes *a forward gain* over the condition prevailing before illness'.[5] Here we can contrast health and healing in their fuller senses with the notion of a medical or surgical cure, in which the normal expectation is, at the most, to return to one's previous state, as when recovering from pneumonia or coming through post-operative debility. We see the essentially biblical nature of these perspectives in, for example, the account of Jesus and the woman 'who had been subject to bleeding for twelve years'. He turns to her and says quite simply, 'Take heart, daughter; your faith has made you well' (Matt. 9.22). In this case the Greek verb *sozo* expresses a healing of the whole person, giving the unnamed woman a 'forward gain' over her pre-haemorrhagic condition.

That God is a God who heals is clear throughout Scripture. We see Yahweh's self-declaration at the waters of Marah: 'I am the LORD who heals you' (Exod. 15.26); the psalmist's exultant 'Bless the LORD, O my soul', with a listing of Yahweh's 'benefits', including 'who heals all your diseases' (Ps. 103.2–3); and, in the life of Jesus Christ, a powerful God-centred ministry that heals 'every disease and every sickness among the people' (Matt. 4.23). That the picture is less straightforward and more mysterious and disturbing than this becomes evident once we allow the texts their full impact, since we see, for instance, that Yahweh declares his ability not only to heal but also to inflict the diseases of Egypt on his people if they should be disobedient (Exod. 15.26). With similar emphasis, Job says of the Almighty, 'he wounds, but he binds up; he strikes, but his hands heal' (Job 5.18). And although the impact of Christ's healings was profound in the immediacy, completeness and permanence of the changes he wrought, his was not a triumphalist crusade to make first-century Palestine the healthiest place on earth, so much as an open portrayal of his divine authority and an affirming pronouncement of an 'inaugurated eschatology' whereby the promise of the kingdom is initiated though as yet not consummated. Further, just as the Old Testament points to a 'dark mystery' with respect to healing and affliction, so the foretelling and realization of Jesus' narrative is a blend of victory and apparent defeat, of conquering kingship and suffering servanthood, of, by inference, a theology of power and a theology of weakness.

Healing and sustaining in the Church

This interweaving of a glorious, light-filled hope with the chequered landscape of present reality is written into the story of Christian pastoral care. In other words, the pastoral function of healing threads its way through Church history entwined with, to use Clebsch and Jaekle's term, the function of 'sustaining', a ministry that helps people 'to endure and to transcend' affliction.[6] We thus see, in the earliest days of the Church, accounts of God-given apostolic power to heal the sick (Acts 5.16) and perform 'signs and wonders' (Acts 14.3) on the one hand, and on the other, divine sustenance given in the face of imprisonment (Acts 5.18–19), beatings (Acts 16.22), riot (Acts 19.29–41), and St Paul's unremitting 'thorn in the flesh' – the last offering up, it seems, through its very anonymity, the general principle that God's 'sufficient grace' is available in all situations of prolonged adversity (2 Cor. 12.7–10).

And so, throughout the unfolding story of pastoral care, we observe the continuing enmeshment of the 'forward gain' of healing and the 'holding the line' of sustaining. We see the former in, for instance, the miracles witnessed by Irenaeus in the second century; the founding of hospitals by Basil the Great in the fourth; and the use of herbal medicine by Hildegard of Bingen in the twelfth; the miraculous healings recorded by John Wesley in the eighteenth century; and the fresh outpouring of the Holy Spirit experienced among the people of the Black Forest in 1842 under the pastorship of Johann Christoph Blumhardt. The pastoral function of sustaining is exemplified in the exhortatory letters of Cyprian, Bishop of Carthage, written to the faithful during the Decian persecution of the third century; John Chrysostom's consoling *Letter to a Young Widow* in the fourth century; Luther's *Fourteen Comforts for the Weary and Heavy Laden* (*c.* 1519); and Jeremy Taylor's *The Rule and Exercise of Holy Dying* (1651).

Charismatic healing

It is when we come to the twentieth century that we meet, within a series of Spirit-impelled tidal waves that wash new life into a seemingly desiccated Church, a fresh healing impetus that, amid its claims of 'signs and wonders', is in recurring danger of glossing over the need for a complementary ministry of Christian sustenance. Pentecostalism, rising on a spring tide of revival in 1906, was fed by the twin currents of Wesleyan Methodism and African spirituality; charismatic renewal eschewed Pentecostal denominationalism and penetrated the mainstream churches from the early 1960s; John Wimber's so-called 'third wave' of 'power evangelism' and 'power healing' sprang from his new openness to Pentecostalism in 1978; the possible 'first spray of a fourth wave' came with the Toronto blessing of January 1994, and the subsequent spread of its dramatic, much-debated ecstatic phenomena; and an openness to the miracle of healing was encouraged in Neil Anderson's Freedom in Christ and the New Wine ministries in the early years of the twenty-first century.

It is in this pathway that we meet the carer as 'healer' or 'deliverer' and find a handling of Scripture that tends to adopt a 'this-is-that' hermeneutic.[7] Here, the interpreter is at great pains to explain that a contemporary phenomenon, such as the Toronto blessing, is just what a particular Scripture has predicted. Mark Stibbe, for instance, adopts this approach to the vision in Ezekiel 47.1–12: the four increasing depths of the river that flowed from the temple are identified as the four successive 'waves' of the Holy Spirit's work in the twentieth century and beyond.[8] At a more modest level, Gloria, the charismatic healer we met at the beginning of the chapter, seemed to adopt a 'this-is-that' expectation in her approach to healing – except that in my case, concluding that my situation did not match either Job's or Paul's, she adopted a 'this-is-*not*-that' interpretation!

Let us consider two contemporary ministries as examples of a charismatic approach to release, freedom and healing: New Wine and Freedom in Christ.

New Wine ministries

In the 1980s David Pytches, then vicar of St Andrew's, Chorleywood, longed to see 'the spontaneous expansion' of the Church in Britain. Along with John Wimber in the USA, he looked to the equipping of Christians with the gifts of the Holy Spirit as one of the keys to this transformation. This inspiration led to New Wine's first conference, when 2,400 people met for worship, Bible teaching and seminars at the Royal Bath and West Showground in the summer of 1989. The numbers attending subsequent summer conferences grew from year to year; by 1993 the work among young people had prospered so convincingly that a separate movement, Soul Survivor, was born. In 1995 New Wine International was launched and related activities have since spread through the United Kingdom as well as to ten other countries. After more than ten years at the helm of New Wine, David and Mary Pytches stepped aside in 2001 and John and Anne Coles took over the leadership.

In 2010 New Wine updated its 'vision statement', which includes the following clauses:

- **Natural and Supernatural:** we want to see every Christian using all the natural reason, wisdom and skill that they can, while also learning to *operate in the supernatural gifts of the Spirit* to minister to others in love and power as Jesus did.
- **Now and Not Yet of the Kingdom:** we want to proclaim the good news of the Kingdom of God and to see that *confirmed by miraculous signs and wonders*, while also maintaining grace to all, knowing that suffering will be part of life until Jesus returns and makes all things new.
- **Word and Spirit:** we want to derive all we believe, teach and do from the Bible as the written word of God, while also learning *to hear and obey the voice of the Spirit speaking to us* individually and collectively.

It is clear from the sections I have italicized that the charismatic element of New Wine is integral to its vision and mission. As well as an openness to the miraculous as a result of the Holy Spirit's gifting, there is a more everyday emphasis that is, as we saw in Chapter 2 on biblical counselling, essentially cognitive and behavioural.

The experience of a friend of ours, Penny, is an example of this. She described how, while attending a recent New Wine conference, she felt a strong concern for Terry, a Jehovah's Witness young man she had befriended, in that he seemed unhappy and had severed his link with the JWs. While praying for him at the conference, she heeded the words of the prayer leader that as well as praying for a person she should be willing to meet up with that person subsequently and offer to pray with him or her. When she returned home she found that Terry had gone back to the JWs and appeared happier. Penny offered to pray with him but was at first taken aback when he responded with, 'We can't pray together as I am a man and you are a woman.' 'Right', she said, 'you pray aloud for me, then, and I'll be silent.' He did just that, and Penny felt that at least they were both addressing God!

Freedom in Christ ministries

Broadly paralleling the New Wine ministries in the United Kingdom, the Freedom in Christ (FIC) ministries were founded in the United States in 1989 by Neil T. Anderson, who had previously taught pastoral counselling at Talbot School of Theology in California. Anderson declares that FIC was born out of the brokenness he experienced during his wife Joanne's protracted illness. After her recovery, Anderson moved in this thinking from his work in evangelism, Christian discipleship and general pastoral ministry to question the strong influence of secular psychology on the Church community. As with New Wine, FIC has spread internationally and is now followed in a number of churches in the United Kingdom. Its UK's executive directors since 1999 are Steve and Zoë Goss, Steve becoming international director of FIC in January 2012.

Innumerable 'how to' manuals have been produced by the FIC stable, including the widely used *Steps to Freedom in Christ* by Neil Anderson (revised in 2009), backed by Anderson and Goss's *Leader's Guide to Freedom in Christ* (2009), a 13-week discipleship course 'for every Christian'. In 2010 a friend was given a copy of *Steps to Freedom in Christ* and the book raised a series of questions in her mind. Inevitably, as with almost any systematic 'secret of life' Christian work, I found the material a mixture of constructive and problematic teaching. Generally, the approach has parallels with the excluding biblical counselling we looked at in the last chapter, being:

- strongly **cognitive/behavioural**, urging changed thinking and behaviour in the believer according to biblical principles;
- essentially **prescriptive** in its choice of texts and tending to avoid reference to other elements in the Bible such as metaphor, symbol, the Wisdom literature and narrative;
- primarily **individualistic**, stressing *my* relationship with God at the expense of our body life in Christ.

Given these realities, FIC's approach has many good qualities. These include strong declarations of the loving, tender nature of God,[9] a right emphasis that we are 'new creations' in Christ, wise teaching on forgiving others[10] and useful appendices on countering fear and anxiety.

However, there are also a number of elements that are more debatable and potentially problematic. Often there is a sweeping emphasis on self-determination, such as 'Your freedom will be the result of what *you* choose',[11] which seems to neglect the Bible's stress on the mystery of God's enabling and human cooperation: 'work out your own salvation with fear and trembling; for it is God who is at work in you, enabling you both to will and to work for his good pleasure' (Phil. 2.12–13). Further, the pressurizing tone of some of FIC's checklists, for example on the occult and other religions, can encourage an obsessive introspection that is in danger of questioning the completed work of Christ and the leading of the Holy Spirit. Perhaps the most controversial teaching lies in Anderson's demonology, in which he seems more preoccupied with the devil and his cohorts than the Bible is. He urges those taking his courses to address Satan and evil spirits aloud: in a section with the title 'The Battle for the Mind', he writes: 'You can submit to God inwardly, but you need to resist the devil by saying each prayer, declaration, etc. aloud.'[12] Elliot Miller summarizes FIC's more dubious teaching as follows:

> Controversial components in Anderson's message include not only his teaching that Christians can have demons but also his belief that Christians should speak to the devil, that they must specifically identify and renounce past sins in order to be free of them, that they do not possess a sin nature, that correct self-perception is the key to sanctified living, and that satanic ritual abuse and multiple personality disorder are common problems caused by a vast satanic conspiracy.[13]

Pastoral perspectives

As we saw in Chapter 2 with the split between excluding and integrative biblical counselling, Christians can readily be divided over central issues such as the interpretation of the Bible. Among the more charismatic approaches to healing and discipleship, the balance between Word and Spirit can be particularly contentious, classically where

'Bible only' conservative evangelicals part company with charismatic Christians who are open to 'new things' from the Holy Spirit. Such schisms have deep pastoral implications.

Amy, a church worker at a well-attended city church, shared with me something of the encouragement her involvement with FIC had given her over five years or so. Declaring that FIC 'strikes at the core of who we are', she told me how helpful Anderson's approach had been in her own life and in the lives of others she had counselled within FIC's framework. She gave an example in the release experienced by a young woman who had been sexually assaulted; she had felt 'dirty' but came to forgive her attacker and was empowered 'through the use of Scripture'.

However, at a church attended by a few of our friends, the vicar introduced the FIC system as a blanket methodology for the whole congregation. Traditionally, the church has been a bastion of evangelicalism but now found itself coerced towards the charismatic emphases of New Wine and Freedom in Christ. Without denying that many members of the church experienced a new sense of release and enabling, a great number of the more traditional evangelicals were puzzled and deeply unsettled. While they declared, 'This isn't right. It's too American. We're English!', those who embraced the new patterns of discipleship and worship dismissed such reservations: 'They can't cope with change!' The congregation became split down the middle. The majority of the 'old guard' held on, despite being uneasy with the FIC material imposed on their home groups, but a number of younger, highly experienced and committed evangelicals left the church to seek more traditional biblical teaching elsewhere. The difference in the mindsets of these two different groups is illustrated by Jack, a veteran Christian who was happier with the church's previous emphasis. An elderly woman of the new persuasion turned to him after a service and asked, 'What has God done for you this summer?' Jack replied, 'He's made it rain whenever I wanted to mow my lawn!'

Sacramental healing

In the autumn of 2010 I was particularly low in spirit, struggling with a host of medical conditions that were keeping me housebound month after month. With seemingly little prospect of recovery, our Anglican rector, Andy Bryant, agreed to bring Joy and me Holy

Communion once a month, and he has continued faithfully to do so since. At one of the earliest of these occasions he offered to anoint me with oil, and I gladly accepted. The oil was dispensed in a small receptacle called a viaticum; after the rector had left us, I looked up the meaning of this Latin word. I was disconcerted to see that the definition included the phrase, 'in preparation for death'! Then, reading on, I felt reassured that the oil-filled viaticum is 'more generally, used as provision for a journey'. This latter definition felt right as we faced the continuing daily ups and downs of long-term illness.

This 'anointing of the sick', or unction, is just one of the seven sacraments recognized by the Roman Catholic Church, the others being Holy Communion itself, baptism, confirmation, penance, holy matrimony and ordination. Mark Pearson writes of the sacraments in his comprehensive study *Christian Healing*:

> Christianity is incarnational. It is based on the truth that God, who is Spirit, became flesh in Jesus of Nazareth. Christians should have no trouble understanding, therefore, that God can use physical objects as vehicles for conveying various blessings, including healing. The sacraments are some of those vehicles.[14]

As Joy and I continued to receive communion from and with our rector, I found, after a year or so, that my physical, psychological and spiritual health, in spite of interruptive episodes of angina and vertigo, had extended stretches of improvement. We came to understand that, even allowing for the realities of recurring, long-term illness, God graciously used the Eucharist in, at times, unexpectedly life-enhancing ways. As Andy remarked, gently and good-humouredly, 'There could be a connection!'

Whereas the danger of charismatic approaches to healing lies in sensationalism and extravagant, unproven claims of miracle, the main hazard in sacramental modes is a superstitious expectation that can border on magic: 'If I receive the bread and wine I shall automatically be made better. Faith in God is not necessary. It's the elements that do the trick!' For Pearson, the way forward to a better understanding of sacramental healing is to acknowledge that we know God not only through our minds as we reflect on his ways revealed in Scripture, but also through our daily experience and an acceptance of the mystery of God as in 'observing a sunset, in worship, in an encounter with a holy person'. He summarizes a wise approach to the sacraments:

> What is needed, as always, is balance. Scriptural revelation always judges personal experience, but personal experience helps us understand scriptural revelation in ways that go beyond, but never contradict, what we know in our minds. Or, put another way, God heals as the forms and elements of the sacraments serve as object lessons of scriptural truth and to help our faith grow, but God also uses the sacraments in and of themselves, which is a great blessing, when our minds are tired, weak, or distracted.[15]

Healing ministries re-examined

Bearing in mind Scripture's corrective that we need to consider the interweaving perspectives of healing *and* sustaining, let us look at two aspects of the healing ministries that are seen by many to be especially controversial: inner healing and deliverance.

Inner healing

The Spirit-charged soil of Pentecostalism and the charismatic movement proved fertile ground for the development of **inner healing**, described by Ruth Carter Stapleton as 'a process of emotional reconstruction experienced under the guidance of the Holy Spirit'.[16] The priority given to *physical* healing, especially in the earlier years of charismatic renewal, increasingly acknowledged the claims of a bigger picture for healing in which a person's inner, emotional life was seen as an equally appropriate target for a God-given 'forward gain'. Here there is a certain logic, not least from the point of view of the Judaeo-Christian tradition, in extending the ambit of desired health to include the inner life as well as the physical. Moreover, from the Second World War onwards the progressively psychologized cultural climate, especially in its more analytic forms, inevitably created an atmosphere conducive to Christian stirrings in the direction of the buried past.

To uncover the buried past requires a 'journey back', and this in turn is seen to need an examination of memories. These, of course, may be unreliable, as is often seen in the television series *Who*

Do You Think You Are? Family beliefs about an ancestor may be proved wrong once the archival search is completed: a grandfather thought to have been a faithful husband turns out to have been a bigamist; or a great-grandmother mythically believed to have been 'the life and soul of the party' is discovered to have been a depressive. Memories may not only be incorrect, they may also be deeply buried.

Amelia's story is typical of the uncertainties with which the inner healer or Christian counsellor must live. She was in her mid-thirties when I saw her, for a period of two years or so, and she still mourned the death of her father from a road accident when she was seven. An only child, she grew very close emotionally to her mother and was very upset when her mother remarried, around the time of Amelia's tenth birthday. She seemed to be holding a great deal of anger towards her father for leaving her, towards her stepfather for his 'irritating' habits, towards older men generally, and, as a Christian, towards all notions of God as 'a loving, heavenly Father'. Amelia shared with me a range of brief snatches of 'stories' from the period between her father's death and her early teens, fragments of memory relating to various male friends of her mother's who visited the family home from time to time. These 'episodes' related to the way certain of these men 'looked at' her, and were recounted, although very sketchily, with evident disgust and clearly felt to be sexually abusive. How much of this recall was autobiographical and historically accurate? How much was it implicit and therefore only hinted at through strong present-day emotion and fragmentary 'flashback'? How much was it dissociative and split off from the 'real' Amelia? Or were there elements of fancy and fantasy contributing to the story, perhaps relating to a child's anxieties over maternal sexual activity? Overall, were the recovered memories true or false?

Most of these questions remained unresolved in Amelia's case. All I know is that by the time the period of counselling had to be discontinued, she was less angry and more trusting towards the older men in her life (including her counsellor!) and had experienced a measure of healing in relation to the fatherly, motherly God who, she had grown to accept, loved her and would not betray her.

Agnes Sanford, an American Episcopalian who was one of the first protagonists for inner healing, used a method she called 'healing of the memories'. She has been a powerful influence on later proponents of inner healing, such as Ruth Carter Stapleton, Francis MacNutt, Leanne Payne and Mark Pearson. In this approach, Sanford especially stresses the importance of the Holy Spirit's 'gift of knowledge', initially as a source for self-illumination during 'times of an inner dullness' that may indicate that 'some old unpleasant memory is knocking on the doors of the consciousness'.[17] If a period of listening and self-examination fails to unlock the offending past, she acknowledges that the 'wounds' may be 'so deep that only the mediation of someone else can heal us',[18] through the confessional, the sacrament of penance or through listening and prayer. It is in the last of these that the healer, after exploring any accessible recall of the needy person's childhood, prays for forgiveness and healing, stage by stage back through the memories and beyond – 'back to the time of birth and even before birth', praying for 'the restoration of the soul . . . of the real, original person'.[19]

In this retro-journey, the presence of the living Christ is seen as an essential companion for healing. Sanford describes her own experience of inner healing, prompted by the words of a 'very discerning young woman'. While praying, this woman had become aware of a fear in Sanford that was linked to the eighth year of her life. After a difficult period of trying to pinpoint the past, Sanford began to recall that she had been 'sick with terror' that her father would die at that time:

> I went back to the memories and found that little child and, playing a game in the imagination, I told her that she was loved and comforted and that she would also be healed. Opening thus a door into the past, I took Jesus with me and led Him to her that He might heal her with His love. And being of a sacramental church, I went to Communion service the next Sunday taking her with me.[20]

For Sanford, these were the first stages of a process of inner healing, in which a 'certain fear' had been identified and the possibility of its removal through Christ believed in.

It is in this realm of the **imagination**, used in inner healing to get in touch with the sometimes buried past, that certain Christians raise their voices in warning. They are most vociferous in our first pathway of biblical counselling, especially among the 'Bible-only' proponents.

Dave Hunt and T. A. McMahon,[21] for example, have attacked with all guns blazing. Alarmed at the perceived poverty of biblical reference among inner healers, they accuse the methodology of not only merely offering 'psychological salvation' but also conjuring up images of Jesus that may be more akin to dalliance with the 'spirit-guides' of shamanism than an authentic encounter with the living Lord.[22] The heart of their concern seems to lie with the very act of an imaginative return journey to the obscured past, with a 'visualization' that offers up a 'mental picture' that '*seems* to be real'[23] but, in fact, may be a seductive delusion at best or at worst an opening up 'to demonic influence'.[24]

In the face of such fears it is worth reflecting that God has made us in his image as creatures of potential imagination. First of all, he dreamed up his extraordinary Creation, imagining and realizing its rich and beautiful complexity. At the receiving end of the method of healing of the memories, we can prayerfully imagine ourselves back into the past as long as that journey is Christ-centred and guided by the Holy Spirit. Dan B. Allender, Professor of Counselling at the Seattle School of Theology and Psychology, specializes in helping those who have suffered sexual abuse, and reminds us that in any healing of the past God is ever present:

> The great discovery of the healing journey is that in getting a glimpse of God we see our past, future and present from the perch of an eternal now. God is above time. He is not constrained by clock time. He is ever present. That means the abuse I suffered as a child is 'now' for him. The day of my departure from the earth is 'now.' All is now. All reflects the mysterious goodness of God, even the agony of the cross. My birth, abuse, redemption, and death are all held in his kindness. He holds time in his hand the way a man holds his son's hand as they cross the street. He leads and lets me walk in the safety of his presence.[25]

Healed or delivered?

When Joy and I had our rendezvous with Gloria and friends at Christ Church vicarage in 1979, we were open, as I explained at the beginning of this chapter, towards the possibility of God's healing for my blindness. What surprised us at the time (although I had come across Gloria's approach elsewhere) was that she did not pray for healing so much as for *deliverance*. I described the experience in *As Trees Walking*:

> After some minutes of collective prayer, Gloria rose and came to stand behind me, laying her warm hands on my head. She had seemed rather tense and, perhaps, unnerved by her encounter, but now she prayed with single-minded vehemence. She cried to God for my healing, commanding diabetes, blindness and brucellosis to depart. While she agonised her fingers kneaded into my scalp. We each echoed our prayers in our hearts, reaching out to God in our trust . . .[26]

Here an alternative paradigm of healing seemed to be operating, one that treats disease as an entity to be 'cast out', to be commanded, in the manner of Jesus encountering evil spirits: 'Depart!' Whether or not the imperative form of Gloria's prayer was appropriate in the context of illness, what place, if any, does the so-called ministry of deliverance have amid Christian healing ministries? Does it simply provide another choice among the 'charismatic' techniques of prayer for physical healing or the healing of the memories? Or is there a quite different mindset behind the concept of deliverance, with its implications of the 'battle in the heavenlies' and a sometimes highly elaborated demonology, as we saw in the Freedom in Christ ministries?

The Bible demonstrates a clear belief that evil is abroad in God's world and that the impetus of that evil is ultimately laid at the door of the devil, or Satan, a personalized being dubbed as God's archadversary and hell-bent on leading humankind and its enculturation to destruction. Although reference to this baleful influence is sparse in the Old Testament, the Gospel accounts, particularly the Synoptic Gospels, are charged with a number of significant references to the Enemy and his allies, the evil spirits or demons. The coming of the incarnate Son of God, in announcing the dawn of the kingdom of God, forces the hand of the powers of darkness to a series of pitched battles, each of which is lost to the tempted, resisting and victorious Jesus of Nazareth. The Epistles, although largely shifting their language from talk of demons to the pervasiveness of sin and the dead hand of a law devoid of grace, declare the eternal outcome of the greatest battle of all, fought in Gethsemane and on Golgotha and proved victorious in the resurrection:

He forgave us all our sins, having cancelled the written code, with its regulations, that was against us and that stood opposed to us; he took it away, nailing it to the cross. And having disarmed the powers and authorities, he made a public spectacle of them, triumphing over them by the cross.

(Col. 2.13–15, NIV)

How are we to understand the outworkings of this victory in the deliverance ministry? My own experience of this approach to healing is very limited. One of the few occasions in my counselling when there seemed to be a palpable evil oppressing the life of a client was during the first session of my engagement with Olivia, a single teacher in her mid-thirties who had come to me complaining of 'strange sensations'.

I found her prosaic and level-headed as she shared with me something of her struggles in her relationships with men, including a married friend with whom she'd fallen in love. A few years before, during a very difficult time in this relationship, Olivia had become ill with numbness, muscle weakness and general fatigue. A male colleague suggested that she visit a 'natural healer', Damien, whom he recommended. She made an appointment and arrived feeling both apprehensive and curious. After a preliminary assessment of her muscle strength while she was lying down, to her surprise he asked her to hold a piece of wood over her heart and then asked her, 'In what former existence have we met before?' and added, 'Think back to Africa.' Now feeling alarmed, she sat up and said she did not want to go any further. Armed with two herbal extracts, for 'weakness' and 'stress', she fled the scene, feeling 'heavy, oppressed and depersonalized'.

Six months or so later, Olivia had a series of flashbacks and hallucinations, including a sudden sensation of Damien's presence, making her feel 'uneasy and drowsy', the fleeting strong smell of his herbal remedies, and on another occasion the sound of a voice as she fell asleep, saying 'blackness and bile'. Understandably, she was deeply unsettled by these experiences.

In our following discussion, she shared with me something of her Christian faith and her desire for a church where she could discuss her doubts and questions. We considered a number of practical ways forward, which included suggestions for church fellowship, the recommendation that she buy a Bible, and the need for her to ask

God to show her the way forward. At the end of our time together it felt right to offer to lay hands on her and pray for her release and deliverance from oppression. She readily agreed and I prayed for her.

When I next saw her, six months later, I found her greatly improved though still troubled about her singleness. She now read the Bible frequently and had found a church she liked. She recounted, too, that the morning after I had prayed for her, she retched and vomited, feeling that 'all the rottenness' was leaving her and experiencing a sense of peacefulness that stayed with her for some months.

This episode with Olivia reminded me that there are dark forces that can invade and disturb people's lives, as are seen in the Gospel accounts of Jesus' engagement with needy men, women and children.

Unmasking the powers

I have briefly described the engagement with Olivia with some diffidence since her unfolding story was, in my counselling experience, exceptional. However, how are we to think about such encounters, and more comprehensively, about the 'powers' that the New Testament refers to?

More than any other pathway to be considered in this book, the healing ministries remind us, sometimes too sensationally and obsessively, of the grim reality of evil.[27] Whereas biblical counselling may emphasize 'sin', pastoral counselling 'psychological blocks', spiritual direction 'the shadow' and social transformation 'injustice', the Pentecostal and charismatic spiritualities that undergird many approaches to healing often envision their calling, as we have seen, in terms of a battle with the forces of darkness – with Satan, the archetypal evil one, and his lickspittle servants, the demons or evil spirits. It is here that those influenced by modernist antipathy to the supernatural on the one hand, and those caught up in charismatic renewal or, for that matter, the darker reaches of New Ageism on the other, should take heed of C. S. Lewis' oft-quoted words from the Preface to his *Screwtape Letters*:

> There are two equal and opposite errors into which our race can fall about the devils. One is to disbelieve in their existence. The other is to believe, and to feel an excessive and unhealthy interest in them. They themselves are equally pleased by both errors and hail a materialist or a magician with the same delight.[28]

How can the dark forces, which many in the healing ministries seek to engage with in the name of Christ and in the power of the Holy Spirit, best be viewed as we seek to avoid the polar opposites of dismissive cynicism and obsessive preoccupation? Walter Wink puts the contemporary dilemma well: 'It is a virtue to disbelieve what does not exist. It is dangerous to disbelieve what exists outside our current limited categories.'[29] Writing out of his own personal despair at the suffering he met in Latin America during the early 1980s, he sought to redefine those categories through a fresh examination of the New Testament's insistence 'that Christ is somehow, even in the midst of evil, sovereign over the Powers'.[30]

In the first century, Wink argues, spirits or demons, although 'actual entities', were not so much 'hovering in the air' as 'incarnate in cellulose, or cement, or skin and bones, or an empire, or its mercenary armies'.[31] Further, in today's culture he reasons that 'the "principalities and powers" are the inner and outer aspects of any given manifestation of power', whether it be government or armed forces, the health service or systems of education, the Women's Institute or local church. Although the 'outer form' of such structures is self-evident, they also have an 'inner essence' that can be seen as 'the spirituality of institutions, the "within" of corporate . . . systems'.[32]

Such an 'unmasking of the powers' can provide a sorely needed corrective to many in the healing ministries. Some may have unconsciously sided with modernity and dispelled all notion of evil as an affront to circumspect pastoral practice; others may be hugely preoccupied by an elaborated demonology where evil spirits lurk in every physical illness and psychological setback. Wink, I believe, offers a way forward. On the one hand, his focus on the powers exposes contemporary philosophy's dismissal of 'all spirits from the earth',[33] and on the other, his picture of the pervasiveness of institutional and structural 'spirituality' can help free the demon-obsessed healer from spiritual myopia. In this way, the power and influence of Satan, whether seen as a personal being or as a 'profound *experience* of numinous, uncanny power in the psyche and historic lives of real people',[34] is lifted from the merely parochial and narrowly localized and revealed in terms of its global enormity. Wink's analysis exposes the lie put about by this 'father of lies'. We see this type of deception where, for example,

charismatic evangelists 'try to terrorize us with Satan' while con-
doning systemic evil in the shape of militant nationalism, sexism
or racism.[35]

The way ahead

Throughout this chapter, we have stressed the interweaving of
healing and sustaining, of a 'forward gain' that embraces both a
theology of healing and a theology of suffering. Annie Dillard, in
her beautifully lyrical book *Pilgrim at Tinker Creek*, reflects on time
spent watching a female mosquito feeding at the nape of a basking
copperhead snake:

> Here was a new light on the intricate texture of things in the
> world, the actual plot of the present moment in time after the
> fall; the way we the living are nibbled and nibbling – not held
> aloft on a cloud in the air but bumbling, pitted and scarred and
> broken through a frayed and beautiful land.[36]

Here is the reality of everyday life, a life in which we are 'bumbling,
pitted and scarred and broken', albeit in 'a frayed and beautiful
land'. Paul sounds the same note when he writes, 'For while we
are still in this tent, we groan under our burden' (2 Cor. 5.4); and
again, 'We know that the whole creation has been groaning in labour
pains until now; and not only the creation, but we ourselves' (Rom.
8.22–23).

Wendy Bryant has a background in social work and has worked
in the diocese of Guildford and Oxford to raise awareness, in parish
churches and beyond, towards those who are often seen as 'scarred
and broken' or 'groaning under their burdens', including those
with mental health problems, learning difficulties,[37] disability or
chronic illness. One project that she and her husband Andy set up
was the Pain Support Group, a venture initiated by the Guildford
diocese, the parish church of Worplesdon, Surrey, where Andy was
rector, and a neighbouring parish. Using the latter's parish hall,
four weekly evenings were offered, as a Lenten course, for those in
any sort of pain – physical, emotional, psychological or spiritual.
Unsure of numbers, they anticipated about 30 people; 90 turned up,
indicating a profound level of need. Among these were a number of
middle-aged women who suffered from chronic fibromyalgic pain.

Wendy described the sense of isolation in these sufferers, who would say, 'I dress smartly, I apply my make-up, so that I can relate socially. But, as a result, no one believes I'm in pain.'

The four evenings focused on, respectively:

- three people being interviewed by Wendy, to share their stories of struggle;
- artwork, sculpting and general creativity;
- pain management, with input from the NHS through a clinical psychologist and medical doctor;
- the relation between suffering and spirituality, a session led by the Bishop of Guildford and a hospital chaplain, Elizabeth, who had her own experience of coping with chronic pain.

As well as all this input and sharing, two therapists were available throughout to engage with anyone who wanted their help. The initial series was so successful that monthly meetings were held thereafter, giving a continuity of care. In response to such commitment to those who experience long-term impairment, one of the prime cries from the heart of sufferers is not only that they are misunderstood and unsupported, but that the reality of their lives is not seen as contributing positively to church or community. As Mary Grey, herself suffering from chronic pain, puts it:

> [We have] a deep sense of being marginalized and/or excluded – by both Church and society. Trying to come to terms with the fact that our levels of pain, the whole reality of our lives, seem to mean very little to the wider society, except as being objects of pity or special help. Yet we have a deep desire that our faith journeys are significant for the believing community. We yearn for a sense of recognition, inclusion and some meaningful belonging.[38]

Anna, when I first met her, was in her early twenties and had spent most of her life in a wheelchair. She and her three brothers had grown up in a caring and artistic Christian household and were much cherished by their parents, Guy and Rosemary. Anna, though a bright and lively child, was late in standing and walking, seemed reluctant to run and fell over more readily than her brothers had at a similar age. When she was two the doctors diagnosed a rare form of muscular dystrophy, and her parents were told that she would be confined to a wheelchair by the age of ten and might well die before her teen years were past.

As Anna and I talked, she told me how, in spite of her many physical frustrations, she was determined to make the best of her situation and keep up with the other children. Although by the age of 14 she could barely put one foot in front of the other, her class-mates rallied, making sure she moved from one part of the girls' school to another at their speed. Anna, short-limbed with very thin arms, was a light burden to her eager friends: sometimes she was carried by two others as she sat on a chair, at other times she was borne aloft, piggyback style, or transported in a friend's arms, cradled like a baby.

Later, in a wheelchair, she successfully studied Classics at the local university, supported by fellow students. However, once graduated, life began to fall apart for her. Obliged to live at home with Guy and Rosemary and unemployed, there followed months of unwanted dependence and physical frustration. After a year of trying to find a possible career in drama, Anna was able to take up a series of con-tracts in the world of disabled theatre. In time she moved to London, where she shared a flat with Marjorie, a caring Christian friend who related to Anna in a straightforward and unpatronizing way.

What can be gleaned from stories like Anna's in terms of our quest for healing amid suffering? I suggest we look at our need for others, our need for humour and, most fundamentally, our need for God.

Need for others

Anna's story is brimful of experiences of help from others: her parents, her schoolmates, her fellow students, Marjorie and other friends.

We have all become freshly aware of this 'one-anotherness' in the huge commitment in training, coaching, physiotherapy, nutrition and athletic achievement in the participants of London's Paralympics 2012. The Scottish blind runner, Libby Clegg, is a clear example. She describes how she needs a 'guide runner', someone who is both a friend and a teacher. Of her present guide runner, Mikail Huggins, she says, 'He has to be my eyes. We are attached at our hands, my left one to his right. It's like a three-legged race in some ways. It's like being one person. While we run, he calls out, "Use your arms more", or "Keep your chin up".' Mikail responded with, 'I'm a shadow. I have to mirror everything she does.'

Here is a powerful picture of our need, as we face life's struggles and challenges, of at least one other who is alongside us, giving words of encouragement or being silently supportive.

Need for humour

Quite recently Joy and I celebrated our fiftieth wedding anniversary. We gathered with 50 others at a friend's house and extensive gardens on a chill day in April 2012 for lunch and a relaxed and convivial afternoon. Our younger daughter Rache and son Simon together gave a speech before proposing a toast to us. Rache caused a stir as she started with: 'Last night Simon and I discussed what we'd say and I suddenly realized that this is the speech I was going to give at Dad's funeral several years ago!' She was referring to the various medical crises I'd had over the previous decade, almost every year of which the family had talked about 'Dad's last Christmas!'

Following the laughter Rache's opening comments prompted, she declared, 'When Graham and I married, Dad gave the speech and used words beginning with F: Friendship, Faithfulness, etc. Today I'm going to use the F word!' This was followed by a mix of shocked silence and nervous chuckles in the predominantly Christian gathering! She continued, 'And the F word is . . . FOOD!'

Then, true to her style as the deputy head of an infants' school, she produced a linen bag full of slips of paper and asked our intrigued guests to pick one each. Each slip gave the name of a food and these were read out; Rache and Simon then reminisced over family stories concerning pork chops, lemon mousse, 'Christian' biscuits (visitors' special biscuits dubbed 'Christian' by our offspring!), choc ices and other delights.

One anecdote stood out. During the two years of my struggling with blindness, I had two operations on my now sighted right eye. Within this time I did my best to engage with a little modest housework, making the most of some minimal peripheral vision. Feeling especially virtuous one day, I tackled a formidable pile of washing up. This included a large, unexpectedly heavy plate that I lifted from the kitchen table and plunged into the suds. To my horror, my hands closed in on an entire fruit cake which, I belatedly realized, Joy had left for the children on their return from school! All was not lost, though. When Rache arrived home she asked, 'Dad, what's the fruit cake doing draining on the dish rack?' 'All is well, love,' I replied, 'the fruit cake's become a sponge!' This was just one of many episodes during my blindness when humour unexpectedly rose up to give good cheer amid the many deprivations and frustrations.

Need for God

One of the richest metaphors for the pastoral carer who offers healing amid suffering is that of the wounded healer, here the Jewish story of the Messiah who has already come and is to be found sitting among the poor at the gates of the city. All have many wounds in this picture; but whereas the others unbind their wounds all at once and then rebind them, the Messiah unbinds and rebinds his wounds one at a time, so that he is always ready to meet the needs of others. Henri Nouwen sees here a symbol of the pastoral carer, who is both a wounded minister and a healing minister, one who needs must attend to his own 'wounds' of loneliness and isolation and yet, at the same time, is available to bring healing to others through hospitality and community.[39]

During my time of blindness a good friend kindly read the whole of 1 Corinthians on to a tape for me. As I listened to his voice gently unravelling this epistle and its message of solace in affliction, I became especially compelled by Paul's words in the first chapter. Here the link between the sufferings of Christ as wounded healer and God the Father's sustaining love in our times of need is powerfully expressed:

> Blessed be the God and Father of our Lord Jesus Christ, the Father of mercies and the God of all consolation, who consoles us in all our affliction, so that we may be able to console those who are in any affliction with the consolation with which we ourselves are consoled by God. For just as the sufferings of Christ are abundant for us, so also our consolation is abundant through Christ. (2 Cor. 1.3–5)

In this ministry of consolation (*paraklesis*) we are back once more to the parakletic aspect of pastoral care, a route to meet human need that flows from the 'Father of mercies' and the abundance of Christ's sufferings, through to those who suffer, who in turn reach out to console others who are in any affliction.

Mary Grey, Emeritus Professor of Pastoral Theology at the University of Wales, Lampeter, addresses our collective need for God and one another in the calling of wounded healing:

But in our woundedness we are called to be healers. We are called to minister in mutuality to each other's brokenness. In our recovery of attending and tending to the lost rhythms and connectedness we are healers of each other. We re-discover 'care' through this recovery of connection. We are heard out of the depth into speech . . . by a listening of the heart, not by the speech of the expert. We minister to each other . . . through a kind of mutual messianism, where we participate in the relational, redeeming energy which was manifest in the life, death and resurrection of Jesus of Nazareth.[40]

It is these themes of relating, heart-listening and community that will provide the focus for our three remaining pathways: pastoral counselling, spiritual direction and social transformation.

4

Pastoral counselling:
the maturing person

———————◆·●·◆———————

> Only in the continuous encounter with other persons does the
> person become and remain a person. The place of this encoun-
> ter is the community. (Paul Tillich)[1]

Josh and Eileen, young parents with two small girls, regularly attended
the local church. They came to see me in a pastoral context in order
to try to resolve their many differences, which in turn led to bickering
and misunderstanding. The couple presented with strongly opposite
personalities: Josh came across as someone who resorted to a logical
analysis of a situation and he admitted that he found it hard to express
his feelings; Eileen, in contrast, talked readily of her 'feelings, desires
and wants'. In their latest row, over the delay in Josh putting up shelves
in their bedroom, he said he felt criticized by Eileen, whereas she
declared that she wanted to help him but felt rejected as he'd say she
'didn't do things the right way'.

During the early weeks of their coming to see me they both shared
something of their family backgrounds. Josh said that his parents, who
lived nearby, never 'talked about or expressed feelings', yet his mother
still treated him like a child, saying such things to him as 'Make sure
you wear a scarf, dear, it's cold.' The dynamic in Eileen's family was
more complex, in that her father had never shown her affection once
she moved beyond childhood, but her mother had overcompensated
for this lack of affirmation by 'spoiling' her daughter. Josh had grown
up with the belief that you deal with life by keeping your own counsel,
being level-headed and treating the showing of emotion as suspect.
Eileen, experiencing her mother's emotional closeness and lavish spending on her behalf, engaged with life fully and, at times, extravagantly.
She admitted to low self-esteem, tracing this back to her father's cold-
ness towards her in her teen years and young adult life. She indulged

in comfort eating, and as a result was overweight, and she was harried by Josh for her compulsive spending on more and more new clothes.

I saw the couple over the next three months with regard to their struggles to understand and value each other, and then Eileen alone for the following year or so to address her low self-esteem and explore ways to encourage her towards a greater self-acceptance. As always in any counselling enterprise, there were ups and downs for both Josh and Eileen in terms of progress towards greater stability and understanding in their lives together as husband and wife, as parents, as friends to others and as Christian disciples in their local church and wider community. Overall, Josh learned to declare his feelings more readily and to be less critical of Eileen, not least in their attempts at DIY around the house, and she moved forward, in fits and starts, in controlling her spending and overeating, and, more fundament-ally, in her valuing of herself as lovable and loved.

In many ways, it is neither the excluding tendencies of those within biblical counselling, nor the ecstatic highs of those within charismatic renewal, that provide the patient listening and empath-etic understanding required in stories like Josh and Eileen's. It is in our third pathway of pastoral counselling that, rightly perceived, there is the special capacity for coming alongside the broken, disillusioned and anxious and making some sense of life's disorder and disease. We will explore this pathway under the headings of pastoral counselling, the maturing person, and the way ahead.

Pastoral counselling

In Chapter 1 we were reminded that contemporary pastoral care inherits a long history of the Church's 'cure of souls', in which 'helping acts', carried out by 'representative Christian persons', are 'directed toward the healing, sustaining, guiding, and reconciling of troubled persons'.[2] We saw, too, that today's pastoral care seeks to be egalitarian in its calling (lay and ordained, women and men), communal in context and pluralistic in its frame of reference. In turn, we established an underly-ing pastoral theology that is committed to case studies, is open to hermeneutics and aims to be liberational. In the last two chapters, we have observed how our first two pathways are linked with certain elements within overall pastoral praxis theologically and psychologic-ally: biblical counselling presents as a directive form of teaching and guiding within the evangelical tradition; and the healing ministries are, at their best, an interplay of healing and sustaining within charismatic and sacramental understandings. We need, now, to see how our third pathway, pastoral counselling, meshes with the traditions of pastoral care and the insights of present-day theology and psychology.

Definitions

In Lewis Carroll's *Through the Looking-Glass*, Humpty Dumpty scornfully says to Alice, 'When I use a word, it means just what I choose it to mean – neither more nor less.' And in many ways the term 'pastoral counselling' eludes precise definition in that its remit within pastoral care is ever expanding.

At root, the adjective 'pastoral' evokes biblical imagery of God as shepherd of his people, and a long history, through the Latin for shepherd, *pastorem*, of Christian pastoral ministry. Although many have jibbed at the word's intimation that God's people are like sheep, passively and unthinkingly following the flock's instincts, 'pastoral' is better viewed as a reminder of God's call for us to follow the Good Shepherd in a loving, 'eyes wide open' relationship.

The noun 'counselling' immediately brings the notion into the twentieth and twenty-first centuries and the pervasiveness of 'secular' psychology and therapy in contemporary society. Even so, the term 'pastoral counselling' often implies both more and less than the sum total of these two words. We can identify at least five uses, indicating the steady widening of pastoral counselling's remit from the 1940s to the present day:

- counselling by the ordained carried out exclusively in the community of faith;
- counselling by the ordained that is available both for the community of faith and the wider community;
- counselling by believers, either lay or ordained, within the community of faith;
- counselling by believers, either lay or ordained, that is available for the community of faith and the wider community;
- counselling by people, regardless of their beliefs, in a range of communal and institutional contexts.

Thus expressed, these uses are descriptive of *any* form of pastoral counselling, whichever faith system is involved.

If we take **Christian** pastoral counselling, the prime focus of this chapter, we can see the practice of our first two mini-definitions in traditions that strongly emphasize ministerial authority, and the next two in churches that countenance the 'priesthood of all believers'. The fifth usage is increasingly common in a pluralistic society where the caring and personal tones of the word 'pastoral' have been reclaimed in a number of organizational settings, including schools, universities, hospitals and 'secular' counselling centres.

As we noted in Chapter 1, there is a close tie in the United States between the pastoral calling and ordination. The Association of American Pastoral Counselors (AAPC), for example, since its foundation in 1963 has taken the route of a commitment to those clergy 'who, having acquired specialized training and experience, have chosen to identify themselves as specialists'.[3] Whereas the vocation of Christian pastoral counselling in North America, whether parochially, in hospital settings or as a specific professional calling, is primarily a call to ordination, it is probably fair to say that in the United Kingdom pastoral counsellors are as likely to be lay as ordained, whether the context is the local church, a Christian counselling centre or the wider community. Americans further recognize **pastoral psychotherapy** as a comparable but more specialized calling than pastoral counselling, which, to quote Don Browning, 'addresses more completely . . . the psychological and developmental obstacles within a person's life which may be impediments to free and confident thinking, decision making, and action'.[4]

With this understanding of the variety of uses of the term,[5] I would like to define pastoral counselling on a comprehensive base, as follows:

> Pastoral counselling is that activity carried out by representative Christian persons, lay or ordained, which aims to help others towards constructive change in any or every aspect of life through a caring relationship, which has agreed boundaries and is accountable to a recognized community of faith or other authorizing institution.

Such a definition emphasizes authorization ('representative Christian persons'); comprehensiveness among counsellors ('lay or ordained'), those helped ('others', implying individuals, couples, families and other groupings) and counselling focus ('any or every aspect of life'); the relational and contractual nature of the counselling ('agreed boundaries', pointing to some understood arrangement between the parties in terms of time, place, duration and frequency of contact); and the accountability of the counsellor within the wider context of pastoral care (the local church, Christian counselling centre, settings in school, college or hospital).

Psychological roots

It is as we explore the psychological roots and theological climate of pastoral counselling that we see its historic distinctiveness from the two pathways to wholeness so far examined. Whereas we have noted, with respect to theology's view of psychology, a more 'excluding' stance among biblical counsellors and, by implication, many within the healing ministries of charismatic renewal, pastoral counselling has characteristically adopted a more 'assimilative' position (see pp. 23–4). As we have observed in biblical counselling and among the healing methodologies, and will discuss in the case of pastoral counselling, all three of these pathways – and indeed the whole five that this book considers – can move to a more truly 'integrational' theological and psychological viewpoint.

Thomas C. Oden has been one of the foremost commentators on the failure of nerve within the tradition of Christian pastoral care in the face of the rise of secular psychologies and the consequent rapidly growing 'counselling movement' from the 1930s onwards.[6] He has charted the slippage from a pastoral theology at the dawn of the twentieth century that was healthily cognizant of its rich biblical and pastoral heritage, to a posture adopted by mid-century that had, under the newly erected banner of 'pastoral counselling', brushed aside the historic traditions for an eager celebration of a new-found faith – a Freudianism that replaced sin with neurosis and a Rogerianism that discarded God-dependence for a heady bid for human autonomy.

Similarly, Anton Boisen's warning of the impending dangers of an uncritical assimilation of the psychoanalytic mindset went largely unheeded, and throughout the 1940s Boisen's heirs encouraged clergy to cultivate the insights of Freud and his successors. This trend towards the psychologizing of pastoral care and counselling was reinforced by the publication of Carl Rogers' *Counseling and Psychotherapy* in 1942, a work that quickly became a standard textbook in many theological seminaries. At this time the influence of Seward Hiltner and his *Pastoral Counseling*, published in 1949, came to the fore. Once a student of Boisen's, Hiltner increasingly held fast to the essentially church-based and pastoral aspects of pastoral counselling. In the 1960s Hiltner was in the vanguard of the opposition to the specialist concerns of the American Association of Pastoral Counselors (AAPC), arguing that private pastoral practice, cut off from the community of faith, was a contradiction in terms.

Inevitably, assimilative tendencies towards secular psychology travelled across the Atlantic to British shores through the return journeys of such London-based Christian pastors as Leslie Weatherhead and William Kyle in the 1950s and 1960s respectively.[7] Even so, as with Hiltner, these two practitioners sought a measure of integration of psychological and theological insight and aimed to hold the linkage between pastoral counselling and the wider work of the Church. In 1969 Kyle founded the Westminster Pastoral Foundation (WPF), a body committed to church-based pastoral counselling, at least during its first six or seven years. By the 1980s, however, WPF's increasing psychotherapeutic sophistication led to a crisis of identity between its Christian pastoral roots and the overt secularization of its highly esteemed training programmes. David Black, writing in 1991, records WPF's decision to move its focus from the pastoral to the clinical:

> a new argument has prevailed: that, indeed, what is done and taught at WPF is not pastoral counselling. WPF, which now trains few clergy, is teaching and practising a secular activity to which the word pastoral has no application. Consonant with this, the word has been dropped from our official description of the work we do, which is now called psychotherapy or psychodynamic counselling, and is retained in our organisational title only to maintain continuity with our roots.[8]

The founding of WPF, along with the formation of other influential pastoral counselling bodies in the 1960s and early 1970s such as Frank Lake's Clinical Theology Association (1962) and Louis Marteau's Dympna Centre (1971), led to widespread pressure for a British national pastoral organization that would provide a platform for communication and debate, and become, perhaps at a later stage, a vehicle for standardization and accreditation, with some parallels to the established AAPC. Just as Hiltner had resisted the slide towards professionalization of the pastoral calling in the United States, so a prophetic voice was raised against a comparable trend in the United Kingdom. Robert Lambourne, general practitioner, psychiatrist and theologian, wrote in 1970 that he deplored 'the total lack of theological thrust in the so-called dialogue with psychoanalysis', which he had witnessed during a recent visit to the United States.[9] A year later he declared his opposition to the standardizing, specializing American model and its incursion on to British soil:

> It is not enough to change our concepts of pastoral counselling to bring them up to date with those of the U.S.A. pastoral counselling organisations which though sophisticated and enlightened are trapped in their history of having been formed, and having flourished, under the pressure of clinical psycho-therapy in a highly individualistic society. A model of healthy interpersonal life, of communal life as requiring mutual confrontation and mutual confirmation around the matter of values is essential for pastoral care.[10]

Lambourne went on to urge his British colleagues towards a 'concept and practice of pastoral care which is lay, communal, variegated, adventurous and diffuse'.[11] Here was a bid, against the tide of a psychologized, professionalized and clericalized pastoral ministry, for a recovery of the 'priesthood of all believers', in all its rich variety, interconnectedness and risk-taking commitment to others. Lambourne expressed the strong desire that pastoral counselling rediscover its rootedness in Christian pastoral care, breaking free from a 'hang up' theology[12] that leans heavily on the problem-solving clinical models of medicine and the psychoanalytic tradition.[13]

In spite of Lambourne's warning, a British pastoral organization was set up in 1972: the Association for Pastoral Care and Counselling (APCC), which later became contributory to the formation of the British Association for Counselling (BAC), which in turn became the British Association for Counselling and Psychotherapy (BACP) in 2000. Even so, according to the pastoral theologian David Lyall, 'it can be argued that Lambourne's critique did have an influence upon the issues that became important in APCC'.[14] We shall return later to the continuing debate between the psychological and pastoral rootedness of pastoral counselling.

Theological climate

Just as biblical counselling has been cultivated in the theological climate of evangelicalism and fundamentalism, and the healing ministries in the context of charismatic renewal and sacramentalism, pastoral counselling owes its nurture primarily to liberalism and, latterly, post-liberalism. This is not to deny that many evangelicals, charismatics and sacramentalists engage with the pathway of pastoral counselling. It appears that those who do so are among the more 'open' and 'radical' sections of these stances, essentially because, it seems to me, they are freed up from a 'conservatism' that is tied exclusively to biblical proposition, ecstatic encounter or liturgical means, respectively. Put another way, it is those members of the first two pathways that are more open to the rich variety of divine leading who may, in turn, combine their methods with a more **relational** emphasis, which overlaps with pastoral counselling. The strength of biblical counselling lies in its theology of Word-centred redemption, while that of the healing ministries lies in Spirit-centred sanctification; in contrast, pastoral counselling, where it is most theologically aware,[15] is undergirded by the richly humanizing perspectives of an **incarnational** theology.

First, let me make a brief comment on the use of the term 'liberal' in Christian contexts. Just as the word 'conservative' is often used pejoratively of *other* Christians, from whom one wishes to distance oneself, the same could be said of the use of the word 'liberal'.

Thinking back through my own story of Christian commitment, I recall, during my teen years at a conservative evangelical church, being upset by fellow Christians who dubbed the new vicar a 'liberal', implying that he had strayed from the faith 'once delivered'. I disagreed, finding him godly, caring, wise and deeply committed to sharing with us, at a boys' Bible class, the rich narrative in St Mark's Gospel. Later, at Cambridge, where I was Selwyn College's representative for the Christian Union, I was again concerned at the insularity of other Christians with their dismissive attitudes towards the 'liberals' who attended the Students' Christian Movement. Among the latter were some of my best friends, attractively open and honest, questioning matters of faith freely, expressing their doubts, but nonetheless faithful in their commitment. Since those early days my views have widened, seeking to cross boundaries to a more inclusive mindset, eager to learn the things of God through colleagues and friends of many Christian persuasions: evangelicals, both 'conservative' and 'open'; sacramentalists; a friend who belongs to an Eastern Orthodox church; and, of course, so-called 'liberals'.

As a result, it is one of my aims in this book to seek to dispel something of this compartmentalizing smokescreen by taking seriously the self-declarations of each pathway's advocates.

Let us explore certain of the key elements in the theological climate of pastoral counselling, considering first the liberal tendency, followed by post-liberal trends.

The liberal tendency

The influence of the secular psychologies on pastoral counselling has leavened the lump of liberalism in its theology. Here is an essentially anthropocentric theology that has disturbed the digestive processes of Christian orthodoxy by its questioning of supernaturalism, divine revelation, the veracity of the biblical record and the foundational truths put forward by the faith. At its most optimistic, liberal theology is heady with the notion of humanity's upward, self-achieving progress, purporting a 'gospel' in which, according to Richard Niebuhr, 'A God without wrath brought men without sin into a Kingdom without judgement through the ministration of Christ without a cross.'[16]

Perhaps the strongest theological voice in the developing pastoral counselling movement of the 1950s was that of the philosopher and theologian Paul Tillich. Born in rural Germany in 1886, Tillich grew up in the context of his father's ministry as a conservative Lutheran pastor, his own strong questioning of his father's traditionalist faith, and his deep affection for his more liberal mother, who died of a painful cancer when Tillich was only 17. As a professor of theology, his lectures and speeches brought him into conflict with Hitler's Nazism; in 1933 he, together with his wife Hannah and their daughter, emigrated to the United States, where his academic career blossomed until his death in 1965.

Seeking to comprehend Tillich's theology can feel like trying to discern an unfamiliar landscape through a gathering fog. This is mainly because his language about God and humanity is based on an existential philosophy in which his main struggle is with the concepts of 'existence' and 'being'. He rejects the idea of a personal God, arguing that for him God is the 'ground of being' and 'being-itself'. He declared, 'God does not exist. He is being itself beyond essence and existence. Therefore to argue that God exists is to deny him.'[17] Rollo May described his long-standing friendship with Tillich in his

74

book *Paulus*, reflecting on the absurd questions that, Tillich argued, arise from traditional beliefs in God as a distinct being. For example, in answer to the question, 'How did God spend his time before he created the earth?', Tillich's German students once replied, 'Thinking up punishments for those who ask such questions'![18]

Even though Tillich's theology presents great difficulties for orthodox Christian belief, there are two areas in which he is seen to be especially relevant to pastoral care and counselling. The first of these is found in the title of his best-known book, *The Courage To Be*, published in 1952. Here he analyses the human predicament of anxiety, and offers a way forward through an exploration of a Christian understanding. At the deepest level he sees human need in terms of an **existential anxiety**, which he defines as 'the anxiety of a finite being about the threat of non-being'.[19] Life is never as we would wish it to be, whether this is through experiencing illness, bereavement, depression or worry, and for Tillich we need to muster courage in the face of such threats to our peace of mind.

The second matter that distinguishes Tillich's contribution to the pastoral encounter is his **method of correlation**. Here he seeks to hold on to both philosophy and theology: philosophy asks life's difficult questions; theology offers the answers. In this quest for connection and correlation, let us consider the pastoral situation for Eileen, whose story we considered at the beginning of this chapter.

Eileen had struggled since childhood. At that time her father's affection for her was still self-evident, but as she grew into her teen years he seemed to reject her, calling her 'thick' and 'stupid'. Her mother, in spite of her continuing love for Eileen, seemed to connive with her husband's distancing; frequently she said to Eileen at the time her periods started, 'Don't let Dad know'. This and her increasing weight made Eileen reflect, 'There must be something wrong with me.'

In pastoral counselling, the question arose: How could Eileen's deeply established low self-esteem be addressed and countered? Posed in Tillich's terms: What correlation, if any, could be found in Christian theology in answer to this existential question? It is here that I explored with Eileen the value of reading and reflecting on Psalm 139, whereby she might learn to replace her self-talk of 'I'm hopeless', 'I'm ugly' and 'What's wrong with me?' with statements such as, 'O LORD, you have searched me and known me', 'I praise you, for

I am fearfully and wonderfully made', and 'lead me in the way everlasting'. This, of course, was not a quick process, but over the 18 months or so of her coming to see me she gradually progressed, becoming less dependent on her mother, more valuing of herself and more appreciative of God's inclusive love.

For Tillich, Eileen needed the 'God above God', to use his term – the one who is the 'ultimate source of the courage to be' and is present 'in every divine–human encounter'. He goes on to say:

> a church which raises itself in its message and its devotion to the God above the God of theism without sacrificing its concrete symbols can mediate a courage which takes doubt and mean-inglessness into itself. It is the Church under the Cross which alone can do this, the Church which preaches the Crucified who cried to God who remained his God after the God of confidence had left him in the darkness of doubt and meaninglessness. To be as a part in such a church is to receive a courage to be in which one cannot lose one's self and in which one receives one's world.[20]

Post-liberal trends

Given the sometimes puzzling nature of Tillich's theology and his elevating human autonomy above divine revelation, it is unsurprising that he has many critics. Among these, arguing from a pastoral theo-logical position, Elaine Graham writes that it is Tillich's assumption that theology and psychology converge into one central truth that is the sticking point; this view runs the risk, she argues, 'of refusing any distinction between Christian truth-claims and the faith community, and secular culture'.[21]

Further, as we saw towards the end of Chapter 2, just as the evan-gelical presuppositions of biblical counselling have been more recently challenged by post-evangelicalism, progressive orthodoxy and Robert Webber's 'younger evangelicals', so liberalism has been questioned by a post-liberal trend.

Post-liberalism is a theological movement that began at Yale Divinity School in the late twentieth century. Key figures include Hans Frei, David Kelsey, George Lindbeck, Stanley Hauerwas and David Tracy.[22] In this trend there is a reaction against liberalism's individualism and an embracing of the communal aspects of the human story. There is a fresh engagement with Scripture, with a particular stress on the biblical narrative and the use of that storyline to interpret the world and its culture. Further, where liberalism stresses the primacy of human experience, post-liberalism prioritizes what can be learned through language.[23]

What does post-liberalism have to offer the everyday world of pastoral care and counselling – both through the interpretation of the biblical text and the narrative of 'living human documents'? This can be illustrated by a cross-cultural example.

Emmanuel Lartey examines the cultural and linguistic character-istics of two Ghanaian tribes, the Ga and Akan peoples, and brings their world-views to the scrutiny of the biblical world of the Judaeo-Christian tradition. He unravels the meanings, for example, of the Ga name for God, the 'Supreme Being': *Ataa Naa Nyanma*, where *Ataa* signifies 'father', 'grandfather' or, perhaps, 'person who cares for'; *Naa* 'mother' or 'grandmother'; and *Nyanma* 'nocturnal being' or 'sky'. This 'personified creative life force' is thus seen as 'bisexual, nurturing, eternal and nocturnal (hidden or invisible) and associ-ated with what is above (the sky)'.[24] Such notions of God are caught up with holisitc views of life among both the Gas and the Akans, views that for Ghanaian Christians accord well with the biblical text. Following an examination of the concept of 'wholeness' in the Old and New Testaments, Lartey writes:

> Such a conception of humanity is close to the essence of Akan and Ga humanity. The step from an individual related by spiritual bonds to father, father's lineage and God the Creator and by physical bonds to mother and mother's clan; to an indi-vidual related by spiritual bonds to God and community through faith in the self-giving love and offering of life in Jesus Christ, is a short one. The relationship between them is also plain. Each view enriches the other.[25]

Lartey goes on to show how an acute awareness of the cultural and linguistic contexts of the Ga and Akan peoples needs to infiltrate any pastoral practice among them. He gives the example of the Musama Disco Christo Church (MDCC) of West Africa, which has branches in London and the United States; founded and led by Ghanaians, it offers a pastoral counselling that takes very seriously the ancient traditions of its people, without gainsaying its more recent Christian heritage. For instance, whereas Western missionary zeal attacks polygamy in African society, the MDCC declares that as long as it is allowed by 'the laws of the state', their stance is a permitting one: 'The premise is not to encourage it, but we say that polygamy does not make a person a lesser Christian.'[26] As Lartey points out, Karl Barth's words resonate well with this view: 'we can hardly point with certainty to a single text [in the New Testament] in which polygamy is expressly forbidden and monogamy universally accepted', and where situations arise, 'it would be sheer brutality for the Christian Church to confront men with the choice between baptism and institutional polygamy'.[27] All in all, the MDCC demonstrates a quality of pastoral counselling that is sensitive to issues of culture and language, while seeking not to compromise the essentials of Christian particularity.

The maturing person

Rowena, in her mid-twenties and working as a ward sister, came to see me because she was experiencing panic attacks and persistent anxiety. She and her two brothers felt firmly controlled by their mother, who in turn was clearly under the thumb of her 70-year-old mother. It soon became clear that Rowena suffered from 'separation anxiety'; her father had told her that when she was born she 'cried a great deal immediately', while Rowena herself vividly recalled going on a school 'adventure' weekend at the age of eight, and being frightened when the teachers told stories about 'aliens', afterwards feeling that she never wanted to leave home again. She felt deeply tied to her mother and sensed a 'voice within' that was clearly that of maternal control. She longed to know 'who she was' and to be free of her mother's strong influence. She admitted, too, to being a 'perfectionist', desiring perfect feelings, perfect decisions and perfect relationships. Recently engaged to Piers, a deputy head at the local comprehensive school, she struggled to feel 'right' about him. When she said to him, 'I love you', her inner voice cried out, 'You don't! You don't! You don't!'

It became clear that Rowena and Piers were Christians, and so sometimes our counselling sessions referred to that commitment and its relevance, if any, to her anxiety and battles with her 'inner voice'. Her perfectionism made her extremely worried about not only each day's desires and decisions, but the future. At one point, she asked, 'Will I cope with the next 60 years? I feel I can't!' We discussed at that point the need to take life a day at a time, seeking to respond to the instruction, 'do not worry about tomorrow, for tomorrow will bring worries of its own' (Matt. 6.34). We explored the idea of life as process, a journey and a voyage of discovery and maturing, and engaged with ideas about how 'Mother's view' on life could begin to be replaced by 'God's view'.

Counselling Rowena was a long haul, and at times we seemed to lose our sense of direction, steering constantly into the same backwaters. However, over the next couple of years, within which time she married Piers and had her first child, Simon, she moved into a greater sense of independence from her mother and felt more 'her own person'; she seemed less trapped by her perfectionist leanings and learned increasingly to relax and enjoy being a wife and mother.

We see in Rowena's story, as it unfolded in pastoral counselling, a growing maturity in which she experienced a clearer sense of personal worth and a greater mutuality in her relationships with Piers, her growing son, her parents, neighbours and within her local church.

Let us consider this path towards psychological maturity, using Robert Kegan's notion of 'the evolving self', looking at personhood and maturation.

Personhood

We have already noted the psychological climate that strongly influenced the pastoral counselling movement through the twentieth century. Among such influences, the emphasis on 'the person' in Carl Rogers' method and the stress on the 'autonomous self' in Paul Tillich's theology have been outstanding. The meanings of the 'self' and 'person' have been vigorously debated and innumerable definitions pursued. For me, at times, I would reflect that 'self endlessly defining self, thus evades its essential mystery'.

As we seek to shed some light on that 'essential mystery', we quickly realize that the specialness of what it means to be a 'self' or a 'person' is linked to a balance between **individual uniqueness** and the vital importance of **relatedness**. As Clyde Kluckhohn and Henry A. Murray put it, 'Every person is in some respect like all others, like some others, like no other.'[28] In this statement we have on the one hand the viewpoint said to have been expressed by the Austrian innovative composer Arnold Schoenberg: 'Someone had to be me!'; on the other hand, we have the implied interconnectedness demonstrated in an African perspective by John Mbiti: 'I am, because we are; and since we are, therefore I am.'[29]

Let us explore Robert Kegan's attempt to clarify the maturing process, an approach that pays due heed to both the autonomous and interdependent dimensions of personhood.

Kegan perceives that a fundamental reality of our humanness is to organize meaning: 'it is not that a person makes meaning, as much as that the activity of being a person is the activity of meaning-making'.[30] Further, he adopts a holistic approach to personality that explores 'the need for a sophisticated understanding of the relationship between the psychological and social, between the past and the present, and between emotion and thought'.[31] His balanced understanding of the place of separateness and connectedness in human personhood is summed up well by Joann Wolski Conn's views on Kegan's approach:

> There is never an individual because the word refers only to that side of the person that is individuated or differentiated. There is always, as well, the side that is attached, is embedded. 'Person' refers to the fundamental motion of evolution itself: it is as much about the side of the self that is embedded in a context (family, school, church) as that which is individuated from it.[32]

Maturation

Sadly, as C. K. Barrett has put it, 'Mere lapse of time does not bring Christian maturity',[33] and, we might add, any other form of human maturity; if it did, then all counsellors, pastoral and otherwise, would be out of work. The whole area of human maturation, both what it is and how it might be achieved, is fraught with a multiplicity of theoretical and practical considerations. Broadly speaking, the debate ranges from the more deterministic views that say we are at the mercy of Richard Dawkins' 'selfish gene'[34] to the more activist understandings that declare we can learn from and choose to progress through life's exigencies – as Aldous Huxley has it: 'Experience is not what happens to you, it's what you *do* with what happens to you.'[35]

Pastoral carers and counsellors will be acutely aware that, at a more sophisticated level, the problems of maturation we encounter are often concerned with **an imbalance between autonomy and dependency.** Let me take two examples from my counselling, illustrating these two extreme mindsets.

Benjamin was a resolutely independent businessman in his mid-forties, whose impulse in his teen years, having been out of favour with both his family and his school, was to shout out, 'I'll show 'em!', and whose adult life was being lived out with the strongest of autonomous spirits. He would not take advice, was dismissive of the views of his colleagues and would shout at his girlfriends if they questioned his decisions. In pastoral counselling, there needed to be the aim of helping Benjamin face the isolating nature of his resolute independence and, hopefully, move him towards seeing the value of relationship and connectedness in his personal development. He needed to learn to learn from others.

In contrast to this relentless show of a self-sufficiency that kept potentially intimate relationships at arm's length, Harriet's dilemma lay in her longing for physical and emotional closeness to other people. In her mid-twenties and struggling over 'comfort' bingeing, she was caught in a circle of over-eager desire for company that forced those around her to sidestep her perceived demands, which added to her misery. The goal of pastoral counselling in Harriet's case was to help her see the destructiveness of her desperate clinging to the lives of others. There was, of course, the danger that she would begin to depend too much on her counsellor, so the counselling relationship needed to work through that danger and move her towards self-affirmation and a measure of independence in her friendships.

Robert Kegan confirms this pull between 'differentiation' and 'embeddedness' in his own experience of clients as a therapist:

> One of these might be called the yearning to be included, to be part of, close to, joined with, to be held, admitted, accompanied. The other might be called the yearning to be independent or autonomous, to experience one's distinctness, the self-chosenness of one's directions, one's individual integrity.[36]

Keeping this polarity between connectedness and separateness in mind, Kegan sets out his plan of maturation in the form of an ascending spiral of five progressive stages, each of which is 'a temporary solution to the lifelong tension between the yearnings for inclusion and distinctness'.[37] In his approach, he gives 'equal dignity to each yearning' at whichever stage the maturing person has reached.[38]

Kegan sees the evolving process of maturation as five stages beyond the initial stage of infancy:

(0) **incorporative**: the 'mothering culture' of infancy
(1) **impulsive**: the 'parenting culture' of childhood
(2) **imperial**: the 'role recognizing culture' of school and family
(3) **interpersonal**: the 'culture of mutuality' of late adolescence and young adult life
(4) **institutional**: the 'culture of identity' in love or work
(5) **interindividual**: the 'culture of intimacy' of genuine adult love relationships.

Within these stages there needs to be a progressive discovering of personal meaning and an increasing of connectedness, what Kegan calls 'embeddedness'. Where counselling is needed, the counsellor seeks to join with 'the person in her meaning-making', rather than 'solve the problems which are reflective of that process'.[39]

Let us take just one transition from one culture of embeddedness to another that is commonly encountered in counselling: the move from the 'interpersonal' of stage (3)'s 'culture of mutuality' to the 'institutional' of stage (4)'s 'culture of identity'.

In Poppy's case this transition was proving highly problematic in her attempts to make meaning of her life. Although she lived in a flat with two other young women and worked as a secretary at a local estate agency, she was finding great difficulty in disengaging from the embeddedness of primary relationships, particularly those with an aloof and dismissive father, a mother who was supportive but intensely loyal to her husband, and a married older sister, with whom Poppy had always been compared adversely. Her father had repeatedly told her that she would 'never make the grade' and she had often feigned stupidity to annoy him further. She was torn between longing to be at home with her parents and wanting to stay away from them until they showed that they valued her.

Over the months, a unique row with her mother over Poppy's churlish attitude to her father, and a decision to write to him to apologize for her recent cold-shouldering, seemed to contribute to a less cynical, more understanding attitude towards her parents. Gradually, though with many setbacks, she seemed to nudge in the direction of a greater feeling of personal freedom and an increasing sense of autonomy, encouraged by some new potential friends at the church she was beginning to attend. Poppy was making the transition, however tentatively, from the declaration that 'I *am* my relationships' to 'I *have* relationships'.[40]

It is at Kegan's final stage of 'interindividuality' that we can see something of the flowering of the 'culture of intimacy', the development of a 'psychospiritual' maturity, to use David Benner's term,[41] that is committed to responsible relationships. In Conn's words:

> Maturity is, basically, the deep personal openness which comes from having an independent identity, yet recognizing the personal limitations of independence and autonomy as the goal of development. Valuing, instead, the intimacy of mutual interdependence, the mature person is one who can freely surrender herself or himself, who can risk a genuinely mutual relationship with others and with God.[42]

The way ahead

Pastoral counselling has had a firm place in the history of pastoral care over the past 80 years or so. As we have seen, its original context was strongly influenced by the world of secular counselling. Although its awareness of its calling within the Church, other faith community, hospital, school or college is paramount, pastoral counselling still looks, rightly, towards the basic listening and counselling skills hammered out through research and experience. For a full appraisal of those skills in the context of faith communities, let me recommend Alistair Ross's *Counselling Skills for Church and Faith Community Workers*.[43]

We have explored in this chapter some of the cardinal features of pastoral counselling, including its historic metaphor of the shepherd or pastor, its soft-focus attention to 'living human documents', its aim of psychological maturity and relatedness, and its correlational method, backed by liberal and post-liberal theology. Let us now, in considering the way ahead, briefly visit two final areas of debate: the formative place of Scripture, and the self and salvation.

The formative place of Scripture

What place, if any, does the Bible have in pastoral counselling? We saw in Chapter 1 that pastoral care is a 'soft-focus' activity as it seeks to interpret people's lives, their story, motives, desires and circumstances. And in pastoral counselling this same 'hermeneutic of the life' carries over and the sensitivity of this process often excludes the overt use of Scripture. We see something of this point in the ministry of Jesus. Although he readily quoted the Hebrew Bible in his confrontations with the devil and religious leaders, his everyday response to needy men, women and children was more 'soft-focus'. We see that his recorded encounters with the common people were essentially relational: a look, a question, a touch, a request, a rebuke, a story, rather than a quoted text.

Thomas Oden carries this 'soft-focus' approach into the world of counselling and psychotherapy in *Kerygma and Counseling*, when he writes that 'there is an implicit assumption hidden in all effective psychotherapy which is made explicit in the Christian proclamation'.[44] He further holds that the 'implicit assumption' that is hidden in the effective therapeutic encounter is that the person being helped is not only accepted by the counsellor but is, through Christ, acceptable to God:

> the final power in life is for us, and . . . we are forgiven and acceptable. The Christ event clarifies this assumption. In our prodigality, alienation, estrangement, frustration, guilt, and hostility we find we are still loved by the Father and received into sonship. This divine love is not a reality we discover but a reality that discovers us. We do not win God, he wins us.[45]

A particularly helpful approach to the implicit nature of God's Word in pastoral counselling is given by Donald Capps in *Biblical Approaches to Pastoral Counseling*. Here he looks to 'form criticism', a method of biblical criticism that 'tries to discern the original religious and social needs' that were served by the text's 'form or literary genre, such as saga, folk tale, legend, or prophetic saying'.[46]

A very useful example of his approach is seen in the parallels he draws between the form of the lament in the Psalms and the form of the grieving process.

Most Christian pastoral carers will be acutely aware of the value of the Psalms in bringing solace, encouragement and challenge to those who struggle with life's demands. The Psalter has a gravitational pull for the careworn. During the long months that followed my quadruple bypass in 1993 – months that encompassed the early stages of kidney failure, a pleural effusion, an abscess in the chest wall and a protracted stretch of relentless coughing from brucellosis – my limited attention span and discouraged spirit made reading next to impossible. The only texts that I could encounter – and these in very brief snatches – were Psalms 34 and 116, and just a small handful of their verses seemed to have any staying power. There is no subtlety in the fact that the two that hung most persuasively in my mind were: 'This poor man called, and the LORD heard him; he saved him out of all his troubles' (Ps. 34.6, NIV), and 'Be at rest once more, O my soul, for the LORD has been good to you' (Ps. 116.7, NIV).

Given that every human emotion, from joy to sadness, from praise to the desire for revenge, is represented in the Psalms, it is no surprise that they are of profound relevance to the grieving person – whatever the nature of the loss experienced. Capps points out that over a third of the Psalms can be considered to be in the form of the personal lament,[47] a form that has a great deal to say about how the people faced and overcame their suffering. Walter Brueggemann, in his paper 'The Formfulness of Grief',[48] shows how, in ancient Israel, the experience of life shaped what was expressed to God and the pattern, or form, of that expression in turn shaped experience. In the form of the lament, for example, those who had experienced affliction – through sickness, betrayal or defeat at the hands of enemies – were helped towards rehabilitation and restoration within the community by the 'formfulness' of the relevant Psalm. The function of the form is a forward movement that both gives shape to the grieving experience and defines a response: as Brueggemann puts it, 'The form not only describes what is, but articulates what is expected and insisted upon.'[49]

Capps gives one telling example of the formative place of the Bible in pastoral counselling, wherein our understanding of Scripture implicitly helps shape the unfolding story and process of helping others in need.

The self and salvation

We have seen both Tillich's 'autonomous self' and Kegan's model of the 'evolving self'. It is David F. Ford's *Self and Salvation* (1999) that helps to carry our thinking in pastoral counselling about selfhood to another level, that of the 'redeemed self'. Ford describes a rich progression from the 'hospitable self', through the 'self without idols', to the 'worshipping self', the 'singing self' and the 'eucharistic self'. Throughout the book he powerfully links the story and formation of the self to the formative influence of other selves and, ultimately, to our redeemed selfhood, both individually and corporately, 'in Christ'. Each of us has an identity derived from who we are in relation to others and who we are, created, loved and redeemed by our Trinitarian God.

I am reminded of something of Ford's analysis of 'self and salvation' as I look back at my journal for October 2010. I mentioned in Chapter 3 that I was at the time having a particularly difficult few months healthwise: the continuing battle with chest aches that seemed to be a form of angina, with shortness of breath, attacks of crippling vertigo and reactive swellings of lips and tongue from medication had led to feelings of depression, and at times hopelessness in both Joy and myself. Although at that stage I hardly knew our recently arrived rector, Andy Bryant, it felt right to ask him for help. And so on 23 October he came to listen to my story and pray for me.

It proved to be a very special time, as this wise man, also an experienced Relate counsellor, listened and gently advised. Quoting from my journal:

1 He reminded me of the God who is there in the midst of suffering.
2 That God is gentle and fully understanding.
3 That God's presence can mean God's silence, as in the best friendships where two people are happy with silence.
4 He advised me to breathe deeply when awake at night, to say the Jesus prayer ('Lord Jesus Christ, Son of God, have mercy on me, a sinner') or a short verse from a Psalm.

Following this deeply therapeutic encounter, Andy offered to bring Joy and me communion each month, since I was virtually housebound at this time. After sharing the Eucharist, the three of us would chat together over a cup of tea with 'the rector's special chocolate biscuit' kept for him. In this way the three of us experienced something of the psychological and spiritual healing of the sharing of the 'hospitable self' and the unfolding of the 'eucharistic self'.

David Ford summarizes the individuality and corporateness of redeemed selves in the Pauline epistles as follows:

> There is no need to think of just one face in our hearts: we live before many internalised others. But we do not worship them. Paul's complex naming of God is inseparable from the naming of Jesus Christ as Lord, one in whose face the glory of God is found and who is trusted to relate to all other faces too.[50]

We will explore this transformation of the redeemed self in Christ more fully in our next chapter, as we consider our fourth pathway of spiritual direction.

5

Spiritual direction:
the uncomplicated heart

But I understood at last that God breaketh not all men's hearts alike . . .   (Richard Baxter)[1]

In the last chapter we considered the story of Josh and Eileen and explored something of the process of pastoral counselling in relation to the ups and downs of their life together. We noted that after seeing them initially as a couple, it seemed right to engage Eileen on a one-to-one basis. In this way we made a measure of progress over the two years in all that I saw her for counselling. At that stage she asked whether we could switch from counselling to 'spiritual direction' and I agreed to this. What would this mean in terms of the therapeutic relationship? Would the focus of spiritual direction be any different from pastoral counselling? Would the language we used and the terms of reference of seeing her alter in any way?

Over the following few years, Eileen continued to battle with her low self-esteem and comfort eating but, at the same time, she wanted to address her prayer life, use of the Bible and relationship with God. We were still aware of the psychological factors in her story, especially relating to the dominance of her mother, but the primary focus of our times together was on her spiritual journey. Attending an evangelical church, she often felt out of sorts with the prevailing attitudes and approaches of her fellow Christians. For example, in joining a home group, her love of Celtic Christianity, its prayers and symbols, seemed out of place in the cerebral and wordy atmosphere of the group's Bible studies.

In time, Eileen seemed to move to a richer, more peaceful place, both psychologically and spiritually. She had been greatly helped by attending a reflective weekend retreat, was linked with supportive friends in a prayer group and found her time meditating on the Scriptures very rewarding. Towards the end of my time seeing her, she said that she felt that God does love her and accepts her after all, and in this new sense of security she had been enabled 'to reach out to others without making comparisons'. We agreed to discontinue spiritual direction unless she felt a fresh need for further help at some stage.

These encounters with Eileen leave us with the need to clarify the nature of spiritual direction, our fourth pathway. To do this, I propose we consider, first, spiritual direction's context of a mystical spirituality before looking at spiritual direction itself, and then at practical issues concerning spiritual and psychological maturity and spiritual direction and pastoral counselling, including the similarities and differences between them. Finally, as with our other pathways, we reflect on the way ahead.

Mystical spirituality

Behind the notion of mystical spirituality lies the elusive concept of **mysticism**, the meaning of which has shifted its ground repeatedly within the Christian story. The twentieth-century situation ethicist Joseph Fletcher gave up on any attempt at definition, declaring that 'mysticism is something that begins in mist and ends in schism'![2] Evelyn Underhill, in her classic analysis of the subject, pointed to the 'universality' of mysticism across the religious divides: 'all mystics . . . speak the same language and come from the same country'.[3] In contrast, within Church history we can see the origins of the mystical in the *mysterion* of the New Testament: 'the mystery that has been hidden throughout the ages and generations but has now been revealed to his saints' (Col. 1.26). Here is the revealing of life's secret, an opening up of what was formerly closed, a sharing with all God's people of the *mysterion*, 'which is Christ in you, the hope of glory' (1.27). These Pauline statements exemplify the particularizing voice of a Christ-centred, revealed theology that is the heartland of a fully Christian mysticism. Robert E. Webber defines this spirituality in *The Divine Embrace*:

> The heart of biblical and ancient Christian spirituality is *our mystical union with God accomplished by Jesus Christ through the Spirit*. God unites with humanity in his saving incarnation, death, and resurrection. We unite with God as we receive his new life within us.

Put simply, he adds, Christian spirituality 'is *God's passionate embrace of us; our passionate embrace of God*'.[4] Here the 'divine embrace' infuses new life into us, enabling our response of love and commitment.

However, as we saw in Eileen's love of the mystery in Celtic spirituality and her struggle with the wordy and analytical approach of her fellow Christians, there are two main traditions within Christian spirituality. Although their roots are found in the Scriptures, it was not until the early sixth century that a Syrian monk, who called himself Dionysius the Areopagite, delineated these two ways of trying to understand God.

The more familiar of these to many Christians is that of a **kataphatic** or **affirmative** theology, a term based on the Greek words *kata* (according to) and *phasis* (image). It is a theology full of content and expresses its understanding of God in metaphors. As Belden Lane puts it, 'God is father and lover, judge and friend, raging fire and still small voice – all of these, and yet none of them.'[5] We can see from such images that there are strong elements of a kataphatic theology in the Bible, where we read, for example, 'With all wisdom and insight he has made known to us the mystery of his will, according to his good pleasure that he set forth in Christ' (Eph. 1.8–9), and 'But when the fullness of time had come, God sent his Son, born of a woman, born under the law, in order to redeem those who were under the law, so that we might receive adoption as children' (Gal. 4.4–5).

And, of course, Church history is brimful with an image-filled kataphatic theology. We see this perspective in the writings of Irenaeus in the second century, expressing a spirituality in which 'God's glory is the human person fully alive'; in Francis of Assisi, celebrating the presence of the divine in the sun, moon, stars, birds and beasts; Martin Luther, focusing on the centrality of a theology of the cross; Ignatius Loyola, declaring a content-filled and systematic spirituality that is Trinitarian and Christ-centred; and Seraphim of Sarov in the late eighteenth century, representative of an Orthodox spirituality that celebrates the interdependence of the created order.

The second major tradition in Christian spirituality is that of **apophatic** or **negative** theology, from the Greek word *apo* (away from). Here there is a movement away from image and metaphor in a theology that is speechless before the mystery and hiddenness of God. This apophatic perspective is captured in the story of Moses and Yahweh. For example, when the Ten Commandments had been given him, we read that 'Moses drew near to the thick darkness where God was' (Exod. 20.21). Later, when Moses urges God to show him his glory, the Lord replies with, 'you cannot see my face; for no one shall see me and live.' He then places Moses in a cleft of the rock, saying, 'I will cover you with my hand until I have passed by; then I will take away my hand, and you shall see my back; but my face shall not be seen' (Exod. 33.17–23). Here Moses' view of God is partial and fragmentary: the divine glory is way beyond human comprehension and Moses' speech-making is silenced.

This apophatic emphasis, that God is in some sense 'unknowable', also weaves in and out of the mystical tradition. In the third century, Plotinus, a Greek philosopher from Egypt, emphasized the possibility for the soul to lose its distinctiveness by merging with the One; Gregory of Nyssa, a century later, declared that 'we can have no knowledge of the divine nature, which lies beyond the reach of the human mind';[6] the writings of Dionysius the Areopagite put forward a 'theology of negation' in which 'the soul passes beyond anything it can perceive or know into the darkness where God is';[7] *The Cloud of Unknowing* of fourteenth-century England pursued Dionysius's *via negativa*, wherein 'the most goodly knowing of God is . . . known by unknowing';[8] and the sixteenth-century Spanish mystics Teresa of Avila and John of the Cross declared a spirituality in which the soul needs to traverse the darkness of God's inaccessibility before experiencing union with the divine love.

We will keep in mind this rich inheritance of mystical spirituality as we examine the tradition of its salient pastoral ministry: spiritual direction.

Spiritual direction

Most, if not all, religions have within their framework a place, sometimes centrally, sometimes peripherally, for a 'spiritual guide', a man or woman who is seen to be a repository of a special wisdom, in touch with the divine: the Hindu 'guru', the Buddhist 'master', the 'shaman' of northern Asian and native American traditional religion, and the 'rebbe' of Hasidic Judaism. It is the precursors of the last of these in the Old Testament priests, prophets and wise men and women that have the closest parallels with the genesis of Christian spiritual direction. Guidance is no longer found through magic, the stars or casting lots; it is offered and received, rather, through the mediatorial voices of Yahweh's faithful servants: figures such as Moses, with whom the Lord would speak 'face to face, as one speaks to a friend' (Exod. 33.11), and Elijah, whose commitment to the younger Elisha was such that even at his final departure he could say, 'Tell me what I may do for you, before I am taken from you' (2 Kings 2.9). Such 'go-between' listening to God and nurturing of others is clear in Jesus' handling of his disciples: 'I have called you friends, because I have made known to you everything that I have heard from my Father' (John 15.15); and in Paul's gentle but firm direction-giving to the young Timothy: 'Hold to the standard of sound teaching that you have heard from me, in the faith and love that are in Christ Jesus' (2 Tim. 1.13).

We can discern three main metaphors for the spiritual director in the Christian tradition: he or she is desert-dweller, soul-friend and midwife. Behind these roles stands the biblical ministry of the priest, a ministry to Israel that, according to Walter Brueggemann, 'dealt with the problem of sin and guilt and the felt need for forgiveness and reconciliation'.[9] In each of these three priestly metaphors, the spirituality is a spirituality of presence.[10]

Desert-dweller

One major biblical theme that has proved relevant throughout the history of spiritual direction is that of the desert: tracts of wilderness in which the individual or group is tested to the limits and, through God's grace and power, emerges chastened, refined and obedient. This tradition is seen, for example, in the Sinai wanderings of the Israelites; in Elijah's flight from Jezebel (1 Kings 19); in Yahweh's allurement of Israel 'into the desert [to] speak tenderly to her' (Hos. 2.14, NIV); in John the Baptist's abstemious life as Christ's forerunner; in Jesus' 40-day encounter with the devil; and in Paul's post-Damascus road sojourn in Arabia (Gal. 1.17). David Runcorn summarizes this biblical perspective in his *Spirituality Workbook*:

> The God of the Bible is the God of the desert. There is no path to God that does not pass through the wilderness. There is no significant leader in the Bible whose own spiritual formation did not involve significant times in the wilderness.[11]

We find that much of the sensibility of this scriptural perspective is carried over into the spirituality of the Desert Fathers. Responding, perhaps, to the blunting of Christianity's edge once it became the state religion in AD 312 under Constantine, an increasing number of believers took to the Syrian, Palestinian and Egyptian deserts throughout the fourth century to embrace a life of solitude and abstinence. One of the early precursors of this influx, Anthony of Egypt, stands out for his resolve as a young man to sell all he had to give to the poor, and for the longevity and profundity of his 'desert experience'. Sought out by many troubled Christians for counsel during the 'great persecution' under Diocletian, Anthony was both a chief instigator of the monastic movement and one of the principal prototypes for the long tradition of spiritual direction. Under his influence, 'spiritual fathers' and 'spiritual mothers' became available to guide their fellow pilgrims on their journey with God, using the gift of 'discerning the spirits' to illumine the way amid the warring factions of good and evil. This 'desert' ethos of the solitary 'abba' as director has been handed down through the centuries in both the Western and the Eastern Church. In the latter, for example, the role of the *staretz*, or elder, of Russian Orthodoxy was renewed in the late eighteenth and early nineteenth centuries as a calling to solitude in the 'desert' of the forest, a vocation whose offer of spiritual guidance enriched 'an entire people from the most humble levels to the most exacting intellectuals'.[12]

This desert tradition is the fertile ground for apophatic theology, and its applicability to spiritual direction lies in the discipline of **contemplation**. John Cassian, writing in the fifth century and influenced by the Desert Fathers, defined contemplative prayer as an 'astonished gaze at God's ungraspable nature, something hidden', while Christopher Bryant captures the awe-filled simplicity of this perspective when he tells the story of an old peasant, a parishioner of the curé d'Ars. The priest was intrigued by the old man's nightly visit to the church, where he knelt for an hour and gazed in rapt attention at the altar. When asked what he said in his vigil, he replied, 'I don't say anything. I look at him and he looks at me.' Bryant describes this essentially 'imageless' contemplation as 'looking and loving'.[13]

Lane sums up the desert perspective in spiritual direction when he writes: 'God cannot be *had*, the desert tradition affirms, if this means laying hold of God by way of concept, language, or experience. God is a desert, ultimately beyond human comprehension.'[14]

Soul-friend

Another ancient tradition that impinges on contemporary spiritual direction is that of the soul-friend. We have picked up something of the biblical stress on the divine friendship extended to Christ's followers in John 15.14–17 (NIV): a friendship that engenders love ('This is my command: Love each other'), obedience ('You are my friends if you do what I command') and the transformative effects of shared insight ('everything that I learned from my Father I have made known to you'). In early Irish Christianity, this offer of God's friendship, reinforced by brotherly and sisterly love, was made visible in the *anmchara*, the 'soul-friend'; this person was sometimes a priest, but often a layman or laywoman, who 'was essentially a counsellor and guide'.[15] Here is the notion of fellow pilgrim, one whose discerning and supportive wisdom was so valued that the Celtic saying, 'Anyone without a soul-friend is a body without a head',[16] became proverbial.

Soul-friendship provides an egalitarian model for today's spiritual direction. One young ordinand who anticipated seeing me on a regular basis through her years of theological training jibbed at the authoritarian tone of the term 'spiritual director'. We discussed the question of 'labels' and decided to dispense with them, although we agreed that the idea of 'soul-friend' was the least threatening 'role' and the most indicative of the mutuality of Christian journeying.

Midwife

In the earlier part of my medical career, working in obstetrics on a hospital ward, and later helping to deliver babies in patients' homes and at the local GP hospital, I was aware that, as a doctor, I was most often called into the situation when the natural process of giving birth was in some way going wrong. On the whole, this interventionist role contrasted with that of the midwife, whose prime commitment was that of *being with* the woman in labour, to give support and encouragement, monitor progress and play a crucial, active part in the actual delivery.

Where the medical role is akin to the problem-oriented nature of counselling, the role of the midwife is more comparable to spiritual direction. Margaret Guenther draws out the analogy in some detail: between the questioning uncertainties of early pregnancy and the tentative nature of beginnings in spiritual direction; between the long months of waiting and the need for patience amid the slow germination of God's new life in the believer; between the non-interventionist first stage of labour and the need for the spiritual director to resist premature action; between the active pushing of labour's second stage and the director's encouragement of the directee's 'hard and focused work'; and, finally, between the joy of a safe delivery and a healthy child and the celebration of 'spiritual friends' at the moment of God's richest blessing.[17]

Tilden Edwards takes the same notion, declaring that 'Being a spiritual friend is being the physician of a wounded soul', while the idea of 'midwife' is more accurately descriptive of the process of spiritual direction:

> The physician of souls explicitly is a midwife, providing an environment for the birthing and nourishing of a whole soul. Always in the forefront of consciousness there is clarity that a three-way process is going on: between the midwife, the person struggling/allowing new life to come and take hold and the Royal One whose loving/healing/driving Spirit we would serve, reflect, and enflesh.[18]

A spirituality of presence

In the metaphors of desert-dweller, soul-friend and midwife, we are reminded that spiritual direction is a ministry of presence. The director as desert-dweller is one who has experienced the refining process of solitude – not necessarily as a solitary, in isolation from others, but in what Henri Nouwen calls a 'solitude of the heart', wherein 'a man or woman . . . is able to perceive and understand this world from a quiet inner centre'.[19] The director as soul-friend is one who freely acknowledges the reality of a fellow pilgrimage, a calling that is companionate and open to mutuality, in which both parties are aware of their vulnerabilities and needs and each is willing to learn from the other. The director as midwife is one who knows how to hold back, how to allow the process of generating and welcoming new life to unfold stage by stage, and how to step forward, not to dampen or gainsay the directee's efforts but rather to encourage him or her in the painful business of bearing fruit in Christian discipleship. All three are undergirded by a spirituality of presence, a fellowship of solidarity that, in turn, depends on the ever-present Spirit of Christ. As David W. Augsburger puts it, 'When one is truly there for another, a depth of communication occurs that is beyond words or style, or technique, or theory, or theology. It is presence gifted by Presence.'[20]

Spiritual and psychological maturity

Some years ago, while working in a student health service, I was gently but firmly reprimanded by a colleague in the department of mental health for raising spiritual matters with Trudy, a young student I was counselling. Her father happened to be a renowned American psychiatrist and, as I understood the episode, Trudy had mentioned this aspect of the counselling process to him. He had been suffi- ciently incensed by the matter to ring the relevant head of department at the local university where I was employed. The criticism, on the face of it, seemed to be a valid one, although my exploratory questions had been tentative and, as I had seen it, simply part of a comprehensive approach to her story. Without denying the need for therapeutic sensitivity in many areas of people's lives, not least with respect to spirituality and personal belief, and acknowledging that my enquiry may have exceeded the mark in Trudy's case, this episode is in some ways a simple example of the deep split between modernist, secularized psychotherapeutic and psychiatric practice and the world of religious pastoral practice – between a psychological and a spiritual approach to people in need.

In many ways, the subtext of this book is to address this very split and to argue that, not least in a consideration of the Christian journey to wholeness, a truer and fuller view of our humanity, made in God's image, is to see the fundamental inextricability of psychology and spirituality – and, for that matter, physicality – in all our lives. This is not to deny, of course, that pastoral care may have a stronger focus in one direction or the other: for instance, pastoral counselling and pastoral psychotherapy may concentrate on the psychological issues, the healing ministries perhaps on the physical, and biblical counselling and spiritual direction on the spiritual. But, I suggest, where human life is split and compartmentalized three ways by such methods, then the truncated approaches to people in need may greatly limit their advance towards Christian maturity.

Let us examine the call to a more integrated style by considering the areas of psychospiritual maturity, and spiritual direction and pastoral counselling.

Psychospiritual maturity

Martin came to see me, still struggling over the childhood death of his older brother, Philip, and the powerful impress of his mother's control on his subsequent 'only-child' upbringing. He had spent his life trying to please his mother and fight off various fears about death and disease – the awful possibility that if Philip could die aged seven, surrounded by family love, then he, Martin, single at 47, could equally well succumb at any time to some disease or sudden accident. In the course of counselling, his comparable drive to please God and his fellow Christians, and his attempts to keep fear at bay through prayer and faith, became a powerful theme that paralleled his life story. Were the issues here primarily psychological or were they essentially spiritual? Or were the psychological and spiritual indivisibly bound together? I am sure that David G. Benner is right when he declares:

> our relationships with God are mediated by the same psychological processes and mechanisms as those that mediate relationships with other people. The spiritual quest is, at one level, a psychological quest, and every psychological quest in some way reflects the basic spiritual quest. Furthermore, psychological and spiritual aspects of human functioning are inextricably connected, and any segregation of spirituality and psychology is, therefore, both artificial and destructive.[21]

Benner holds to his concept of **psychospirituality** on the basis of the holism of the Judaeo-Christian understanding of human nature.[22] He puts forward that this wholeness relates to structure and to specific direction. The structural aspect refers to our createdness in God's image and points to the psychological mechanisms and processes that make up everyday human living; the directional aspect alludes to a person's spiritual orientation in life – ultimately, either towards God or away from him. And although the structural and psychological and the directional and spiritual 'are not equivalent', they are closely interwoven and the one can only be talked about sensibly 'in the context of the other'.[23]

We can take the analogy of our created, fallen human nature as a 'glorious ruin',[24] like one of the beautiful monastic shells of Yorkshire or the Scottish borders. Such a building, although fragmented and a shadow of its original splendour, is nonetheless glorious in its ruined state: an incomplete colonnade here, a fractured arch there, still give some indication of the initial edifice's purpose of providing an aesthetically arresting focus for the communal worship of God. Just as the building's structure *can* be studied while denying its directional purpose, so a person's psychological make-up *can* be attended to while his or her spiritual orientation in life is discounted. To do this, *raison d'être* is sacrificed.

What, then, can be said of the maturing process in terms of its psychological and spiritual aspects?

First, we can say that progress as a person is essentially relational, a bid for balance between the desires for separateness and connectedness. Benner makes this emphasis when he unpacks the broad brushstrokes of human development in terms of the psychological and spiritual. Following Maslow's well-known 'hierarchy of needs',[25] in which requirements such as food, drink and shelter must be met at the basic level before people can aspire to 'higher' things, such as aesthetic appreciation and altruistic endeavour, Benner argues that 'until one *has* a self it is difficult to *transcend* self'.[26]

He points out that it is only when we have resolved 'the unfinished business of the self' that 'we can better become aware of deeper needs and strivings'.[27]

It is here that Thomas Merton's notion of the 'false self' and the 'true self' offers another, complementary angle on the shaping of our psychospirituality.[28] For Merton, the false self is that aspect of who we are which is ensnared by the illusion that separateness from God and others is in our own best interest. The true self finds authenticity and freedom in self-surrender, a 'letting go' that is a paradoxical discovery of the true self, which in turn is also the discovery of 'the true God on whom we depend'.[29] This movement from the false, self-deceiving self to the true, self-sacrificing self is seen in human responsiveness to the divine 'missions', in which the Father 'communicates' to us 'His Word and His Spirit'. In Merton's words:

Our inner self awakens, with a momentary flash, in the instant of recognition when we say 'Yes!' to the indwelling Divine Persons. We are only really ourselves when we completely consent to 'receive' the glory of God into ourselves. Our true self is, then, the self that receives freely and gladly the missions that are God's supreme gift to His sons. Any other 'self' is only an illusion.[30]

For Eileen, the movement away from her relentless low self-esteem, constantly comparing herself to others in a negative way and her frequent binge-eating, to a sense that she was loved by God and was at her best as she reached out to others, was a psychospiritual journey from her 'false self' towards her 'true self'.

Henri Nouwen seems to hold the psychospiritual balance well:

Put simply, life is a God-given opportunity to become who we are, to affirm our own true spiritual nature, claim our truth, appropriate and integrate the reality of our being, but, most of all, to say 'Yes' to the One who calls us the Beloved.[31]

Spiritual direction and pastoral counselling

Let us consider two cameo case histories: in the first, Donna comes for spiritual direction; and in the second, Gerry seeks pastoral counselling.

Donna is struggling in her Christian life as a mother of three children under the age of six. Her husband Ken has a demanding job that takes him away from home for at least three nights a week, but does what he can to help with the children at weekends. Donna feels trapped by tiredness, but also wants to make an effort to 'tune in' to God as best she can. She is a strong intuitive and likes to try new methods of prayer from time to time. She hopes that spiritual direction will give her a little space to explore God's will for her during a particularly demanding stretch of her life.

Gerry, single and in his late thirties, is also struggling, but for him the difficulties centre around a series of close friendships that he has had with women, which he feels he has to step away from when they threaten to become 'too serious'. This leaves him dissatisfied, since he longs for intimacy and would like to marry, but is fearful of making 'a mistake'. He has had a good relationship with Christine, a member of the same local church, for 18 months, but he now feels she is becoming 'too fond' of him. This worries him, since she has been very depressed by a broken engagement in the past. He is increasingly irritated by her assumption that they will marry and yet still finds her attractive. He is in turmoil over her and hopes that pastoral counselling will help him resolve the situation.

Following our discussion on psychospirituality, are we to see these two ministries on offer to Donna and Gerry as essentially the same, differing only in their degree of emphasis on spirituality and psychology respectively? Or, given the very different histories of spiritual direction and pastoral counselling – the former within an ancient pastoral tradition, the latter with its twinned roots in pastoral care and the secular counselling movement – are we to see these as two quite distinct pathways with little or nothing in common? As so often with such polarizing questions, the answers seem to lie in a 'both/and' response. Let us seek to clarify the relationship between these two approaches by examining their common ground, before exploring their distinctiveness.[32]

Common ground

We can, I suggest, see three main areas in which spiritual direction and pastoral counselling are similar: they are contractual, relational, and directional.

The openly **contractual** nature of these two pathways is well established. Although both operate in the wider context of pastoral care and the Christian community, engagement with them requires a specific defining of boundaries and ground rules that is essentially contractual. So both spiritual direction and pastoral counselling are explicit in their agreed commitment to confidentiality, the accountability of supervision, the direction of the helping process and the framework of time and place within which that process can take place.

On the details of the last of these there will be characteristic differences. For Donna, a contract is negotiated initially for monthly sessions of one and a half hours with her spiritual director, with the option to move to six-weekly meetings once a helpful 'working pattern' is established. Here the contract is open-ended, although it can be concluded at any time by mutual agreement. For Gerry, embarking on pastoral counselling, the contract is a weekly one, with six sessions of 50 minutes agreed on to start with. It is understood that the arrangement is not open-ended and a concluding appointment will be made at some negotiated stage.

Both these pathways to wholeness are essentially **relational**. Although either can take place in group settings, they are typically one-to-one relationships, set within the agreed contractual boundaries just outlined. The centrality of relating, as we saw in the last chapter, is a particular feature of pastoral counselling and is allowed to influence the therapeutic process through, for example, the use of transference.[33] Nonetheless, spiritual direction is also relational in the sense of offering a companionate soul-friendship as a fellow traveller who is on the same journey. There is potential healing in the caring relationship in both pathways.

For Donna, this enterprise would be a co-pilgrimage of seeking to discern God's will amid the domestic demands of her life. For Gerry, the counselling relationship itself will at times be the focus of therapy, as counsellor and client explore the relevance of other significant people in his life, both past and present, and their impingement on his relating difficulties with certain women friends.

Spiritual direction and pastoral counselling also share a certain **directional** emphasis. Both are committed to the path towards psycho-spiritual maturity, albeit, as we shall see, with different expectations of the route taken. Joann Wolski Conn notes that both counsellors and directors (or 'spiritual guides') are involved in 'a working alliance' that militates against 'another person's well-defended personality'. The defence mechanisms that we surround ourselves with are challenged and, hopefully, broken down, whether it be an unquestioning adulation of a favourite preacher in the context of spiritual direction, or a tendency to always blame others that is disclosed during pastoral counselling. Conn further concedes that both 'pastoral counselors and spiritual guides would agree with their secular colleagues' that the mainspring in the working alliance is 'the human drive toward life and growth', but, rightly, she argues that these Christian ministries seek to go further, extending 'the interpretation to include its ultimate source: the indwelling Spirit of the living God'.[34]

For Donna, the 'living God' aspect of her life is the desired focus of her seeking spiritual direction in the first place. For Gerry, it is likely that, in time, the relational struggles that brought him to counselling will be explored in the wider context of the church community and his own continuing Christian journey.

Distinctiveness

Sometimes, attempting to clarify the differences between spiritual direction and pastoral counselling is like trying to separate out from a spring the water that flows from it. Even so, given that the common ground between spiritual direction and pastoral counselling establishes them as contractual, relational and directional ministries, let us now outline their cardinal distinctions. We can summarize these as the focus of attention, the orientation of the pathway, and the resources used.

It is in their **focus of attention** that we find perhaps the most fundamental difference between these two complementary pathways. In terms of Christian journeying, we can say that spiritual direction focuses on the continuing journey towards God in Christ and through the power of the Holy Spirit. Pastoral counselling, although committed to the same pilgrimage, is more immediately concerned with unblocking the route when the way forward is hindered, disrupted or countered by life's existential and relational problems.

With these different focuses in mind, we can see how requests for these distinctive forms of help can be misplaced. As Conn puts it, in both ministries the 'presenting objective' may need clarification. For example, someone may seek spiritual direction simply because, in her Christian circles, 'everyone who is anyone' has a 'soul-friend': just as it was fashionable in the 1960s and 1970s to have a counsellor, so in the 1980s, 1990s and twenty-first century it can be deemed stylish to have a spiritual director. Another may seek spiritual direction because he would rather put a 'spiritual' label on his difficulties than face his psychological problems for what they are. Conversely, yet another may mistakenly pursue pastoral counselling in the belief that the Christian counsellor will be adept with advice on her prayer life or on recommending a much-needed retreat. Spiritual directors and pastoral counsellors worth their salt will be used to such mismatching and will either be able to contain the person's needs within their own remit or refer him or her accordingly.

On the receiving side of pastoral care, directees may need to move on to counselling for a period within the course of their spiritual direction, and counsellees may be advised to find a director once their period of counselling is concluded. For Donna, the continuing exploration of her Christian journey in spiritual direction may be disrupted, for a time, by a relational crisis with her husband Ken, and expert marital counselling may be needed. For Gerry, once his anguish over his women friends has been faced, understood and, in substantial measure, resolved, regular spiritual direction may become a necessary support as he picks up with his continuing walk as a Christian disciple.

Where the focus of spiritual direction is on the unfolding Christian journey, and that of pastoral counselling is on those problems that impede that journey, the primary **orientation** of these two ministries is towards God and the goal of human maturity respectively. In the past, the remits of these pathways have often interpreted their stance somewhat narrowly. Spiritual direction has been 'concerned with religion, and intrinsically with nothing else',[35] frequently adopting an authoritarian clericalism. Comparably, pastoral counselling has been accused of harbouring a 'hangup theology'[36] and being merely an expression of an 'ambulance syndrome', in which the pastor is simply 'there to pick up the pieces'.[37] However, as we have indicated with Benner's notion of psychospirituality, there is a more holistic emphasis abroad in both these ministries, an emphasis that, nonetheless, does not betray their distinctiveness. Conn puts her finger on the essence of that difference when she writes that whereas those engaging in pastoral counselling 'seldom pay explicit and consistent attention to the theological dimension of their alliance', those seeking spiritual direction 'always pay explicit and consistent attention to God's presence'.[38]

For Donna, God and his ways with regard to her busy, exhausting motherhood are the initial orientation of her spiritual direction. Whatever the detail of her working alliance with her director, that orientation towards God will always be primary. For Gerry, struggling between his desire for independence from his women friends and his longing for connectedness, the orientation of pastoral counselling will be towards the greater maturity of interdependence, both with his fellow human beings and with his God.

One of the hallmarks of both spiritual direction and pastoral counselling is a sharing of inner states, a process that is facilitated by a range of **resources** in both ministries, including dream diaries, journal-keeping, letter-writing, painting, sculpting, role-play, music, silence and meditation.

My own journal-keeping has been intermittent at times, although in the years following my bypass, as I struggled with slow recovery and the persistence of chronic brucellosis, a flu-like undulating condition that sapped my already weak energies, the entries were more frequent and at times intense. Looking back at that period, I vividly remember the occasion of the entry for 5 December 1994, 18 months after the heart surgery. It reads:

> Yesterday (Sunday) I read some of Nicholas Wolterstorff's *Lament for a Son*[39] to Joy – and as I read tears rolled down my face. What or who did I weep for? For the tragedy of lost youth (Wolterstorff's son, Eric, dying at 25 on a mountain in Austria)? For my lost youth (being held back from teenage adventures at 17 with the onset of Type 1 diabetes)? For my son Simon (also a mountain lover and thus identifying him with Eric)?

A few days later I was able to share this initially puzzling reaction with Anne Long, my spiritual director at that time. She helped confirm my deep sense of loss through years of struggling with ill health, and her encouragement resonated with Isaiah 40.27–31, which I had reflected on that morning. I'd written in my journal: 'the young will soar; the not so young will run; the positively old (and brucellotic) will walk!'

Journal-keeping and the other methods mentioned above are, ideally, undergirded and shot through with a primary resource, that of **prayer**. But it is here, once more, that we see a distinction of emphasis between spiritual direction and pastoral counselling. Both may be committed to the pervasiveness of prayer, but, characteristically, this dimension is handled differently in the two pathways. Conn points out: 'Sharing one's deepest feelings and thoughts as they occur in prayer is often the focus of conversation in spiritual direction'; although all other aspects of life may be included in the working alliance, prayer is of special pertinence 'insofar as it mirrors or affects one's relationship with God'.[40]

In contrast, pastoral counselling will rarely be centred on the prayer life of the client with that degree of intensity, although its relevance to psychological and relational struggles will not be denied. Even so, many pastoral counsellors will keep an open mind on whether or not to pray with the client at the various stages of the counselling process. Here, the temptation to 'magic away' complex issues or to soften the impact of newly acquired insight by a formulaic approach to prayer must be resisted. And yet there may be times when a shared moment of prayer will help a client find solace or encouragement in his or her continuing engagement with the maturing process. Spiritual direction is woven around a core of prayer; pastoral counselling is sensitive to prayer as an invaluable adjunct.

Donna, within spiritual direction, discovers the need to set aside her previously treasured times of daily quiet and prayerful solitude for an exploration of 'practising the presence of God' amid the distractions of the delights and demands of her children; she is encouraged, too, to consider the possibility of a silent weekend retreat, while Ken engages with the less-than-silent children. For Gerry, although he would have 'run a mile' if his counsellor had offered to pray with him during the early weeks of counselling, he is more than happy to request prayer for courage later in the process, once he has decided that he will share his clarified feelings and thoughts with Christine.

The way ahead

Gary Moon and David Benner, in *Spiritual Direction and the Care of Souls*, point to the profound value of the rediscovery of spiritual direction and its God-directed leavening of other pathways to wholeness:

> Spiritual direction offers twenty-first-century Christians an ancient and time-honoured relationship of accountability and accompaniment for walking the Christian path. It provides a place within which we can know ourselves as we are truly known. It gives us a place to meet God. And it also allows both psychotherapy and pastoral counselling to do what each does best while attending to the inner life of persons and learning from their sister soul care profession.[41]

I would like to suggest two metaphors for the way ahead on this path of self- and God-discovery: that of the 'face' and that of the 'heart'.

'Till we have faces'

C. S. Lewis, in his retelling of the story of Psyche and Cupid, portrays the poignancy and power of the face as intrinsic to a sense of self.

Orual, one of the king's daughters, although struggling over her physical appearance, is entranced by the beauty found in nature and declares, 'Who can *feel* ugly when the heart meets delight? It is as if, somewhere inside, within the hideous face and bony limbs, one is soft, fresh, lissom and desirable.'[42] Following a series of trials, Orual resolves to be veiled for the rest of her life as 'a sort of treaty made with my ugliness'.[43] Now the queen, her encounter with deity leads her to the question, 'How can [the gods] meet us face to face till we have faces?'[44] Finally, it is the awe-inspiring countenance of a silent god that leads to Oruah's declaration to him, 'Before your face questions die away . . .'.[45]

Here is a profound insight into what it means to be human before God that has implications for every aspect of our being and relating. It is in the unveiling of our faces, and in the encounters with others face to face, that the depths of human respect, understanding and compassion can be fathomed. The phrases we use around the word 'face' imply the quest for openness, realism and focus: 'facing' a difficulty, an enemy, the future; engaging with 'face-to-face' dialogue; 'facing up' to my shortcomings; and, colloquially, of a situation or person that feels confrontational and intrusive – 'in your face'.

Earlier in this chapter, we encountered Moses and his realization of the mystery and unknowableness of Yahweh. Even so, as Moses returned from Mount Sinai bearing the 'two tablets of the covenant', he 'did not know that the skin of his face shone because he had been talking with God' (Exod. 34.29). In fact, this facial glow was too much for the Israelites to behold and so Moses veiled his face in their presence, only removing the veil when speaking with the Lord. Paul takes up this theme, demonstrating that this 'glory of the face' within the old covenant is now set aside in Christ through his Spirit, leading to a new unveiling:

> And all of us, with unveiled faces, seeing the glory of the Lord as though reflected in a mirror, are being transformed into the same image from one degree of glory to another; for this comes from the Lord, the Spirit. (2 Cor. 3.18)

Just as Orual was changed through her face-to-face encounter with the silent god, so we are transformed as we gaze into the countenance of Jesus Christ. David Ford, though, admits that the concept of the face of Jesus is fraught with vagueness. Even so, he carries over this uncertainty into an admission that the face of Jesus Christ 'transcends simple recognisability . . . and stretches our capacities in the way in which God does'.[46] Here is a face that 'attracts trust, adoration, love, joy, repentance, attentive listening and ultimate hope'.[47] And this facing spills over into all our facings:

> There is no need to think of just one face in our hearts: we live before many internalised others. But we do not worship them. Paul's complex naming of God is inseparable from the naming of Jesus Christ as Lord, one in whose face the glory of God is faced, and who is trusted to relate to all other faces too.[48]

This facing of oneself, of others in our lives and, supremely, our transformative God is written deeply into the nature of faithful spiritual direction.

The uncomplicated heart

Sister Margaret Magdalen, Sister Provincial of the Community of St Mary the Virgin, Wantage, was one of the main speakers at the Swanwick Conference for Pastoral Care and Counselling in 1994. The conference was in early January, ten months after my quadruple bypass, and my mind was still vividly recalling that time of a near-death experience on the intensive care unit. During the conference I had received spiritual direction from Anne Long and she had shared her thoughts with me on the simile of my heart operation and the metaphor of God as 'heart surgeon'. Knowing of my struggles over single-heartedness as a Christian, she had left me with the psalmist's prayer: 'Unite my heart to fear you, O God.' It was hearing Sister Margaret Magdalen's address during the conference's closing Holy Communion that brought together Anne's spiritual counsel and my own reflections, for her sermon's theme was 'The Uncomplicated Heart'.

And it is this notion of the uncomplicated heart that, I believe, is the essential goal of psychospiritual journeying. The concept is as old as God's bid for human love; it resonates in Yahweh's challenge to Israel, 'You shall love the LORD your God with all your heart, and with all your soul, and with all your might' (Deut. 6.5), and Jesus' exhortation to his followers, 'store up for yourselves treasures in heaven . . . For where your treasure is, there your heart will be also' (Matt. 6.20–21).

Annice Callahan and others trace such 'spiritualities of the heart' through the unfolding story of the Church:[49] in the Christian discipleship of, for example, Augustine of Hippo, whose 'long conversion' was gradually translated 'into a single-hearted desire for God'; in Catherine of Siena in the fourteenth century, in whom the heart of the crucified Christ drew out the responsive love of her own heart; in Martin Luther's prayer for a 'clean heart', created by God (Ps. 51); and in the Salesian spirituality of Francis de Sales and Jane de Chantal in the early seventeenth century, with its emphasis on relational love among human beings and towards God, mediated through the loving heart of Jesus.

Here the 'heart' is the personality's 'centre of gravity', the very core of a person's being, and it is in contemplation, much Catholic spirituality argues, that the uncomplicated heart moves towards psychospiritual maturity. Although this contemplation may be 'active', wherein through the use of reason, imagination, the arts, prayer and liturgy a person enters into joyful, attentive encounter with God, it is in 'passive' contemplation that Christian mystics such as Merton see the quintessence of the divine engagement – a 'vivid awareness of infinite Being at the roots of our own limited being'.[50] Once again, we meet the apophatic tradition of Christian spirituality.

Bringing together the threads of Benner's psychospiritual route to human maturity, Merton's call to a selfhood that can only be 'true' as it surrenders to God, and a contemplative commitment to 'an uncomplicated heart', we can look to Annice Callahan for an essentially christological perspective on the mystical pathway to wholeness:

A spirituality of the heart is necessarily incarnational and holistic. It views the heart as a uniquely human reality that is both corporeal and spiritual. It represents the total mystery of the human person. It reflects on what it means to be human in the light of what it means to become divine. A spirituality of the heart is also redemptive and unitive. It describes a particular way of living the paschal mystery in our daily lives, that is, accepting the sufferings and joys that we and others experience. It is concerned with what can unify our fragmented selves, with what can heal our brokenness. It points to communion at a deep level, heart-to-heart.[51]

And so we have, in the metaphors of the face and the heart, two pictures of the transformative journey in Christ that spiritual direction can nurture. Let us now turn to our fifth and final pathway to wholeness, social transformation, reminding ourselves that all psychological and spiritual maturity entails a movement outwards to the environmental, communal and political aspects of people's lives.

6

Social change: the reformed community

Thus says the LORD of hosts: Render true judgements, show kindness and mercy to one another; do not oppress the widow, the orphan, the alien, or the poor; and do not devise evil in your hearts against one another. But they refused to listen.

(Zechariah 7.9–11)

It all began with Claire. Vimla, a young Christian woman from India, had read of Claire's need as a single mother with a small baby, living in bed and breakfast accommodation at a hostel for the homeless in an affluent part of the city; after a great deal of heart-searching, that she might be misunderstood as a 'Lady Bountiful', she resolved to visit her. It was just before Christmas and Vimla was particularly moved by Claire's struggle to save up to buy presents amid a suburban environment that seemed engulfed by festive plenty. The hostel was a veritable rabbit warren, temporarily consisting of around 50 units, housing single parents, men on remand, drug addicts and families with small children – all sharing two small galley kitchens. One family of two adults and four children typified the cramped lifestyle of many. They had been in the hostel for over a year, living out their lives in one room, the size of an average 'living room'. Mealtimes highlighted their plight. An extended journey up and down stairways to and from one of the tiny kitchens entailed a difficult choice: whether to leave the children unattended in a sometimes hostile environment or to risk their presence in the kitchen amid the dangers of communal cooking. Further hazards lay in the return to their room, negotiating the crowded corridors and stairs with hot saucepans of food, all to vie for the one place to eat – sitting on their bed. As Vimla said to me, 'Here, there was nowhere to have an argument, to have sex, to watch TV.'

110

Although Vimla had worked previously in psychiatric settings and with the homeless, she was freshly struck by the level of unmet human need. Her own children were aged two and four at the time and she asked herself repeatedly: how would all this be for me? Her initial desire to help was met in her encounter with Claire; Vimla was able to give her the family travel-cot and assisted in her move from the hostel into more adequate accommodation. However, Vimla had seen a great deal more than just Claire's plight. She had identified a particular dilemma among 'bed and breakfast families': the need for somewhere for the children to play, so that both parents and their offspring could find some respite. She told Linda, a close friend at the church she attended, that she needed 'to do something', and Linda duly linked Vimla with Sophie, a new church member who had considerable experience in childcare provision.

And so these two women pooled their compassion and their expertise, and prayed, trusted and acted. They spread out a map of the city and charted all its bed and breakfast hostels. But where could they find a suitable centre for children and parents to have sufficient space to relax and enjoy a welcome break from their claustrophobic lives? The answer was provided by a woman called Lucinda. Vimla had read in a local paper that Lucinda had recently bought a redundant church with the object of setting up a community centre. The church was located on the map and was found to lie at the pivotal point of the clustering of hostels. Lucinda's response was simple and encouraging: 'Someone said to me only this morning, "You ought to run something for children from B & Bs".' Seeing the site, Vimla and Sophie declared it to be 'perfect'. Looking back at these happy 'coincidences' nine years later, Vimla said, 'God was preparing the way. Our responsibility was just to walk that way.'

The church that Vimla and Sophie attended housed a large, affluent congregation – one to which Vimla, with her radical, 'hands-on', streetwise background, felt ill fitted. Yet suddenly this body of professional and business people seemed the perfect resource for the money, skills and equipment that the play centre needed. Vimla admitted, 'It was our fault for not using all this.' She stood up in church and announced the potential centre's needs, and was overwhelmed by the response: not only with all the furnishings and play things needed

and with the ready covenanting of money, but with the volunteering
of a small army of women – social workers, nursery nurses and young
mums with small children of their own. The project was up and
running.

But, it was asked, would the people come? Vimla had seen enough
of how bed and breakfast parents felt – depressed, lacking confidence,
unable to negotiate with the world outside the hostel – to know that
it would take great courage to venture out to an unknown place,
and to unknown people. Health visitors were mobilized to spread
news of the centre and the city council agreed to send out details
of its impending opening with the weekly housing benefit cheques.
When the day arrived, Vimla, Sophie and a handful of supporters
paced up and down in their eagerness to welcome parents and
children – and practically nobody came. And so a new phase had
to be entered. Three or four women, all with children of their
own, agreed to start the long haul of regular visiting. Each picked
a hostel or two and, all alone, bravely went from door to door. As
Vimla put it, it was less threatening for often suspicious and fearful
'bed and breakfasters' to be visited by a woman, especially one
who knew first-hand what it is to have small toddlers around your
feet all day and to experience frightened or ill babies in the middle
of the night. The team of visiting women were able to say, 'We'll
go with you to the centre,' 'We'll take the children to give you a
breather,' or, confidently yet perhaps unsure of the solution to a query,
'Sure, I could deal with that!' These personal contacts became the
most important element in this venture of communal care. In fact,
not least among those families who never ventured to the play centre,
the regular visits by Vimla, Sophie and the team – simply 'fellow
women' – were the highlight of the week, since so many of them,
once homeless, had been completely shunned by their families and
former friends.

This example of a bid for social change illustrates the main
themes of this chapter: a pastoral practice that is attuned to issues
around gender, culture, politics and the environment, and a pastoral
theology that is essentially liberationist, as we saw in Chapter 1.
To this end we will look at the following themes: a feminist pastoral
theology, intercultural pastoral care, society, politics and pastoral
care, and ecology and pastoral theology, before considering the
way ahead.

Peter Selby makes the case for this examination of the communal aspects of pastoral care when he writes: 'To presume to care for other human beings without taking into account the social and political causes of whatever distress they may be experiencing is to confirm them in their distress while pretending to offer healing.'[1]

Gender and feminist pastoral theology

In 1986 I attended a residential conference at Manchester University on pastoral theology and chose, for one of the workshops I attended, the subject of 'feminist spirituality'. I was somewhat taken aback on seeing that the group comprised about a dozen women and me. It was the time when, yet again, the matter of women's ordination had been sidelined by the Anglican Synod, and there was a simmering of understandable anger among the majority of women present. I listened through much of the hour, feeling privileged to hear the others' discussion and yet wondering whether my male presence was felt to be intrusive. Towards the end of our time together I was asked, 'What do you think, Roger?' and I groped for some sort of response; I referred to Genesis 1.27, saying something like, 'God created us in his image; male and female he created us. And I long for the time when our equity as God's co-image-bearers is truly acknowledged.'

This occasion typified the stark reality of gender issues and the prime need for a feminist pastoral theology in the face of deeply entrenched patriarchal attitudes in church and society. Let us examine this form of liberation theology, considering in turn feminism, feminist pastoral theology and feminist hermeneutics.

Feminism

In the late 1980s I gave a lecture on my book *Roots and Shoots* to lay and ordained pastoral carers in Bristol. The material was brimful of the 'big names' in the history of psychotherapy and counselling, a litany in which Freud, Jung, Rogers, Maslow, Perls and others were discussed. At one point I was interrupted by a young woman social worker, who said, 'Where were the women in your story?' Somewhat shamefacedly, I could only come up with the names of Anna Freud and Karen Horney. Here was an example of the comparative silencing of women, both historically and in my presentation.

Nicola Slee, in *Women's Faith Development*, defines feminism as:

> a political and personal commitment arising out of an under-standing of the structural inequality that pertains, and has per-tained throughout all known history, between the sexes, such that men, as a group, have exercised power and control over women as a group, with the result that women's knowledge, experience and history have been systematically repressed.[2]

This repression of 'women's knowledge, experience and history' is not only true in wider society; it can also be laid at the door of the Church and its theologizing. As Zoë Bennett Moore puts it:

> So many conferences, so many bibliographies, so much Christian teaching simply bypasses the cries and silences, the experiences and the exclusions, the revelations and the confused ques-tionings of the women who make up the major part of most Christian communities.[3]

The voice of feminism, though united against male sexism, has many tones and pitches, ranging from Marxist and atheistic, through 'womanist', in which black American and developing world women seek justice, to various religious groups, including Christian – liberal, traditionalist and evangelical.

Feminist pastoral theology

In Chapter 1 we saw something of Elaine Graham's 'transformative Christian practice' and noted its liberationist bid for social and polit-ical justice, including its commitment to the feminist agenda. Bennett Moore follows Graham's approach, seeking to bring together '*pastoral, feminist* and *theological* perspectives'.[4] She summarizes her methodology as follows:

> Feminist pastoral theology starts with practice, not with theory; is mutual, not paternalistic or clerical; is gender sensitive and eschews sexism; is political and structural, not individualistic; is pluralist and dialogical, not authoritarian. Feminist pastoral theology is an advocacy theology, but also values critical reflection ...[5]

The story of Claire, Vimla, Sophie and other women with which we started this chapter illustrates this feminist pastoral theological approach. Here was a caring theology that started with practice, was mutual in its even-handed commitment to fellow women, sought to tackle the structure of the bed and breakfast world with all its inequities, and offered an advocacy on behalf of deprived women and their children at the local church and newspaper.

The central issues in Bennett Moore's feminist pastoral theology are those of violence and embodiment.

Violence and abuse against women come in many forms: physical, psychological, structural (as with Claire and other women on the verge of homelessness), religious (as in female circumcision and forced marriages), or through the silencing of women's voices in the workplace, the boardroom or within the patriarchal attitudes of many church congregations. In the last of these, notions of male headship, for example, can easily slide into a 'bracketing out' of women's experiences, opinions and gifts, neglecting Paul's injunction: 'Be subject to one another out of reverence for Christ' (Eph. 5.21).

Embodiment is integral to many women's stories and experiences. Issues around body image, lesbianism, eating disorders, the menstrual cycle, fertility, rape and abortion are often the focus of feminist pastoral theology and practice. Heather Walton, in an article titled 'Passion and pain: conceiving theology out of infertility', offers a tenderly written account of her experience in hospital where she and other women were admitted for the investigation of infertility. One of her fellow patients was a minister's wife, with damaged fallopian tubes, who was offered in vitro fertilization. Walton writes: 'I already know that this woman would accept any miracle, any intervention by the hand of God; but not this one.' Learning of her own more puzzling infertility, Walton reflects on the encounter with the medical and nursing staff:

> But I too am left with a riddle. 'You can of course conceive, but you do not in fact conceive.' Perhaps I am possessed? They say 'to you too we can offer the exorcism of IVF. We have no weaker medicine today.' I detain them with questions which they cannot answer and they are impatient to move

on . . . I go to embrace the minister's wife. She has no problems about weeping in the arms of a feminist. We are all together here.[6]

Here is a feminist pastoral theology that is mutual, sensitive to gender and embodiment, narrative-based and deeply compassionate.

Feminist hermeneutics

Elisabeth Schüssler Fiorenza has pioneered an approach to the biblical text that is both deconstructive and reconstructive.[7] In the quest to rescue women's voices from the pages of Scripture, she reads 'between the lines' of seemingly patriarchal texts and interprets 'against the grain' of the narrative. She offers a fourfold hermeneutic:[8]

- a hermeneutic of suspicion towards the text, which is suspected of a strongly patriarchal mindset;
- a hermeneutic of proclamation that seeks to clarify those passages which threaten to hold women in continuing subjection (as when a battered wife encounters Jesus' call to take up her cross); and to highlight those texts that transcend the Bible's androcentrism (as in Christ's first resurrection appearance to Mary Magdalene);
- a hermeneutic of remembrance in which 'new models of interpretation' enable the reader to perceive women at the centre of 'the biblical community' without forgetting their attendant 'suffering and struggles';
- a hermeneutic of creative actualization that aims to take the biblical stories and retell them in the light of a feminist critique.

Such an interpretive approach to Scripture can focus, for example, on the story of Hagar in Genesis 16 and 21. It is here that most exegetes will concentrate on the 'with-the-grain' stories of Abraham and Sarah. Hagar, like so many women throughout history, is pushed from pillar to post. Socially she is marginalized, since she is of servant 'class' and is Egyptian rather than a privileged Hebrew. Sexually she is disempowered and has to submit to the plans of her owners. Physically she is abused, flees for her safety and is eventually rendered homeless. And yet, as Mary Grey points out, 'she was one of the first mothers of a promised child, who received a revelation from God':[9]

encountering the angel of the Lord, she declared, 'I have now seen the One who sees me' (Gen. 16.13, NIV).

It is the interplay between the stories of such as Hagar, Vimla and Claire and biblical interpretation that is the quintessence of feminist pastoral theology's ability to cross the boundaries of gender, class and race. Reflecting on her time spent in Manchester, Heather Walton writes:

> I walk through the streets of Moss Side and a thousand-and-one women's stories leap to heart and mind and soul. Some are easily linked by my scriptural imagination to the precious stories of tradition. Others are not, but still demand their place within a developing Christian pastoral narrative. They are stories relevant to us, owned by us, and useful to us, and they must be told . . . women's voices must be heard.[10]

Intercultural pastoral care

Sunita, a married Gujarati Indian with three children, had been on the receiving end of visits by Sophie, who in time became one of a number of trusted 'fellow women', along with Vimla. Sunita and her husband Justin had both been made redundant at the same time. Justin, like many men who lose work in their prime, felt as if he'd been 'kicked in the teeth' and was determined to make ends meet by setting up his own business. However, the couple's loss of regular income and the large outlay needed for a new enterprise meant that they gradually fell behind with their mortgage payments. Around Christmas, when Sunita was due to have her second child, the building society began proceedings to reclaim their property. The couple appealed against the decision and made every effort to find the needed money for a 'significant reduction in the arrears'. Now with two children, they were unable to put off the evil day beyond the following autumn. Sunita was ticked off by the man at the local housing advice centre for not approaching him before, as she and her husband could have been on the council housing list a year sooner. But no one had told them this. 'Where do we go?' she asked, and was told that no arrangements could be made until the family was out on the street. Telling me her story, she added, 'When you're homeless, you're treated like a criminal.'

On the day of the removal from their much loved home, their seven-year-old son asked, 'Mummy, where are we going to sleep tonight?' As she replied, 'I don't know,' she felt the first pang of a betrayal of his trust in her. She had always been there for him, always as honest as she could be with him, and now she did not have the answer to the most basic of a child's questions. That night's destination was to be the hostel where Vimla had first met Claire. The family were allocated two rooms: one for Justin, Sunita and the baby, and one for their son – distressingly, not adjacent to the parents' room, but about six rooms away on the opposite side of the corridor. Sunita and Justin's room was jam-packed with just a bed, a cot and a wardrobe, a far cry from how one health visitor defined adequate living in conversation with Vimla: 'You can't be a family unless you can sit round a table and eat.' And so began the long haul of cramped living, sharing a remote kitchen and a bathroom with a host of other families, running the gauntlet of neighbours who included men on police bail, a wife-beater and drug addicts, and trying to protect their son from a violent and foul-mouthed environment. Small wonder that he declared, 'I don't like it here,' and applied himself to help his mum count the days for the duration of the 13 weeks they had been given as a deadline for their stay.

It was during their time at the hostel – which eventually proved to be six months – that Sunita picked up a note pushed under her door. It was from one of Vimla's friends and gave details of the newly opened play centre. Understandably, given their raw experience of people in their proximity, when Sophie appeared at the door soon afterwards Sunita declined the invitation. At this time, Sunita remembers feeling so depressed that she would sit, motionless, on the bed all day, nursing her baby daughter. Sophie faithfully kept up her twice-weekly visits until one day Sunita decided to break from her reverie and give the play centre a try. After months of an imprisoning and dehumanizing existence, which lacked the simple necessity of a chair to sit on and the luxury of coffee with milk (they had no way of keeping milk fresh), Sunita broke down and wept at the gentle, genuine, normalizing welcome she received. Here she was treated 'as if normal, by normal, non-patronizing people'; she was surrounded by room to walk in and turn round in; there was generous space and lots of toys for the children; and best of all, she had a seat to herself and a cup of coffee *with* milk.

Returning from the play centre, Sunita cried for much of the rest of the day. Since her childhood in Gujarat, when she had reached out to the 'untouchables' in the village, she had 'always been of help'. And now, in her 'B & B prison', she 'felt no purpose'. Somehow, though, Sophie, Vimla and their friends had rekindled Sunita's generous spirit. Unaware of their Christian commitment, but deeply impressed by the warm humanity of the women at the play centre, she began to talk with the people along the corridor, instead of brushing past them. She felt that there must be something she could do; and eventually she began to help by interpreting for them the bureaucratic jargon of letters from the council, writing replies for them, and offering to look after one of their children from time to time.

Once she, Justin and the children had moved to their council house, her renewed vision for others' needs led to her continuing involvement with the play centre. Her harrowing experience of homelessness had opened a rich vein of practical compassion for her fellow women in similar plight. Her articulate and lucid style led to many speaking engagements throughout the city, wherever churches and other bodies were willing to bend an ear towards the homeless and deprived. These commitments culminated in a meeting at the city centre where Sunita recounted her story to a packed, and visibly moved, assembly of members of parliament, councillors and business people. Now a mother of three, the latest project of this former village girl from India, who happened to be fearful of heights, was a parachute jump for the play centre!

Sunita's story is an example of pastoral care in action, embracing feminist, social, political and intercultural issues.

Emmanuel Lartey, in his book *In Living Color*, sees the limits of cross-cultural and multicultural styles of care in their tendency to stereotype racial groups and individuals. While cross-cultural pastoral care can slip into the danger of a 'them and us' attitude, over-emphasizing difference, multicultural pastoral care, with its surveys and questionnaires, can be trapped by mythic beliefs about categories of people: for example, 'the angry, underachieving Caribbean male; the Asian young woman's oppressive cultural role; the aggressive Muslim; or the problems of the Asian extended family system'.[11]

In the place of these two approaches, Lartey puts forward an **inter-cultural** style of pastoral care and counselling, which follows the dictum 'Every human person is in some respects (a) like all others (b) like some others (c) like no other.'[12]

The stories of Vimla and Sunita and Justin illustrate simply their shared humanity, along with Claire and Sophie and the others involved. They are 'like all others'. All experience similar desires, longings, hopes, frustrations and griefs. Pastoral care needs to be aware of such common bonds, applying as much to the carer or counsellor as the person cared for. Here there is mutuality and a shared vulnerability.

In this narrative, we can say that Vimla and Sunita share certain strong similarities, such as a common origin in India, together with shared understandings of culture, custom, food and ritual. They are 'like some others'. Similarly, Claire and Sophie have the bond of being 'white' women, living in an urban environment with shared values, language and perception of family norms.

And yet, of course, each of these women is unique. They are 'like no other'. Sunita had her own story as a village girl in rural Gujarat, while Vimla hailed from an affluent and intellectual background in the city of Mumbai. They have their own individual tastes, sense of fashion, preferences, physical presence and psychological make-up.

And so in intercultural pastoral care and counselling, these three aspects of the humanity of both carer and cared for are kept in mind: a common humanity made in God's image; cultural distinctiveness within which there are similarities; and individual uniqueness. Lartey sees such pastoral encounters as a **kenotic** activity. He looks to the example of Jesus Christ who 'emptied himself' and 'humbled himself', obeying God 'to the point of death' (Phil. 2.5–8), and urges pastoral care to follow this path of self-emptying:

> It is my view that the time has come for the essence of 'pastoral care' to be freed from the captivity of its 'selfhood' in terms of origins, in order that it can engage in real terms with the pluralism of the current world. Will it by so doing lose its essence and identity? I think not, for it is in such self-emptying that its true being-in-the-world may be realized. It is in giving its very self that its truest goals will be achieved. Pastoral caregivers need the humility and trust in the divine presence that will enable us not to hold on tenaciously and obsessively to the

symbols of office. Instead will flourish an 'other' directed practice that respects difference and seeks to give itself away in loving service.[13]

Society, politics and pastoral care

Tina Hodgett is a pioneer team vicar in the parish of St Peter and St Nicholas' in Portishead, a rapidly growing community of 22,000 and rising, ten miles west of Bristol. Known in the parish as 'team pilgrim', she is one of four clergy, the others being team rector, team pastor and team curate. She started her job in the summer of 2011, and her work was designated as 70 per cent in the community and 30 per cent in the two local Anglican churches.

The period since Tina took up her post has been one of walking the parish, engaging with local activities, establishing networks of connection, hatching creative ideas, praying and, above all, listening: to God and the people of Portishead. Here is an example of 'doing theology', of a praxis that involves the pastoral cycle we considered in Chapter 1: a sequence of experience gained within the community; of exploration of the issues observed; a reflection on such matters; and action in responding to perceived communal agendas, followed by further experience and the beginning of a new cycle.

This process necessarily engages not only with individuals and family units but also with societal structures and local political perspectives. For example, early on as team pilgrim, Tina 'barged in' at the council-run children's centre, where there was a class in progress for immigrant mothers of pre-school age children in the English language. Although the teachers were initially suspicious of this dog-collared intruder, they soon came to respect Tina's previous experience teaching modern languages and her clear commitment to helping the mums from Eastern Europe, Morocco and Syria adjust to a new language. Seeing their need, too, for greater integration in the community, Tina organized a team of volunteers from the church, matching them individually as language partners to meet up with their designated mum and help with the nuts and bolts of everyday speech. For one woman, who was particularly restricted in her home and had few opportunities for exposure to others in the town, Tina suggested she take time out between 3 and 4 p.m. to watch CBeebies, with its commitment to instruct children in learning English!

This doing theology in the community is a liberation theology that parallels feminist, intercultural, two-thirds world and, as we shall see, ecological theologies. Sallie McFague says of these radical approaches:

> As with all theology, they emerge out of a concrete, social context; they identify what they believe the central vision of Christianity to be; they offer particular insights, insights that emerge in part because of special perspectives – insights that ought to be seen as illuminating to all people ... The crucial difference between these new theologies and classical theology is that for the first time they are coming from women, from people of colour, and from the poor.[14]

Here we can consider the classic metaphor for liberationist pastoral care as that of the **prophet**. The prophetic voice is of the essence in God's call for social reformation and transformation. Waldemar Janzen sums up the distinctiveness of the prophetic call as a contrast to other callings:

> It is different in the case of the prophets ... a prophet could in no way ask others to emulate his or her 'prophetic life.' It was peculiar to the prophetic calling that it was uniquely addressed to certain persons by God. One could not aspire to it as a way of life or imitate those thus called.[15]

In many ways, Tina's calling is that of a prophet. She is placed in a role that works against the grain of contemporary society with its prioritizing of achievement and measurable results. It is not an easy place to be, as she finds when she reflects on how she spends her days, in contrast to the packed diaries of her three colleagues. Also, however friendly she is, she is often treated with suspicion as she gently gatecrashes mums' groups or a nursery class, is seen walking the highways and byways of the town, or seeks to play pool with drinkers at a local pub. It takes time and courage to win confidences and live 'the good news' amid other people's busy lives.

Martyn Percy takes the notion of 'the ecclesial canopy'[16] as a metaphor for the relationship between society and the Church's prophetic call. His understanding of this concept includes these elements:

- The Church provides 'an overarching narrative of meaning and truth in modern life'.
- Its 'ecclesial canopy' is a form of 'stretched social skin' that 'provides shape and identity for the wider social body'.
- The canopy 'provides social and cultural space' for society to explore the values that make for its 'social flourishing'.
- The space the Church provides can lead to an exploration of ideas and values 'in a spirit of generosity and openness'.[17]

In the face of society's secularization, consumerism and preoccupation with the media and information technology, the Church's ecclesial canopy can be a profound source for kingdom values, a spring that refreshes a parched land. Here boundaries can be crossed and divisions healed. As Percy puts it: 'the ministry of Jesus is rooted in God's charity – a radical commitment to challenging divisions, and bringing about forms of equality that amounted to a nascent form of politically-led pastoral theology'.[18]

Ecology and pastoral care

Transition Portishead[19] is a locally based commitment to raise awareness of 'the twin problems of climate change and peak oil' and organize projects 'around the themes of food, energy, and recycling', as well as 'running a programme of workshops with local schools'. Tina, the local pioneer team vicar we met above, made links with this body in 2011. Once more, there was suspicion and some puzzlement that a local cleric was showing interest in this 'low carbon' project. What has the Christian faith, of all things, to do with ecology? In time, though, attitudes softened. One of Transition's supporters attended a supper party at the church, when overseas contributors to the meal brought along their national dishes to eat together, and everyone watched the opening of the Olympics 2012. Tina was so impressed with the big screen used that she got in touch with Transition's chairman, Jon Gething, who organized an evening at St Peter's in January 2013, when Professor Jonathan Bamber, head of the Bristol Glaciology Centre, led a discussion that included the showing of 'On Thin Ice', the final episode of the BBC's *Frozen Planet* series, highlighting the accelerating loss of Arctic ice. Here church and community are combining with the common agenda of being good stewards of the Earth's depleting resources.

David Atkinson, with his background in science and theology, has presented in his book *Renewing the Face of the Earth* a powerful case for the reality of global warming, the impoverishment of the created order through human greed and the need for the Church to wake up to its creational calling. He and others have pioneered Operation Noah, a Christian organization that 'provides leadership, focus and inspiration in response to the growing threat of catastrophic climate change endangering God's creation'.[20] Atkinson writes:

> Climate change is real, is growing, and has potentially very dangerous consequences for the well-being of the planet and for human life. I shall argue that a Christian theology of creation celebrates the interconnectedness and interdependence of all creatures within God's cosmic covenant, in which humanity has a significant responsibility to care for and protect the rich variety of species within God's created order. We particularly have a special responsibility for other human beings. The people most affected by climate change will not be in the USA or the UK. They will be living in the poorest and most disadvantaged parts of the world, as indeed they are today.[21]

And one of the most disadvantaged parts of the world is the Thar Desert in northwest India's Rajasthan. Mary Grey, her husband Nicholas Grey and Ramsahai Purohit, a follower of Gandhi, founded a small NGO, Wells for India, in 1987 in response to Rajasthan's drought, in which 60 million animals died. This work has continued since, embracing the drought of 1991–2001 and the continued desertification over the following years. In *Sacred Longings* she highlights the effects of traditional patriarchy, globalization and climate change on the impoverished women of Rajasthan. Here Grey puts forward an **ecofeminism**, which 'focuses on the lost connection between the domination of women and domination of the earth'.[22] She lists the environmental and socio-political factors that combine to devastate the lives of Rajasthan's women, including:

- India's industrialization and neglect of village life;
- climate change causing increasing drought and desertification;
- the prioritizing of cash crops like sugar cane and cotton, which in turn demand huge amounts of water;
- India's vast dam schemes backed by the World Bank;
- increasing tourism with its demand for showers and swimming pools.[23]

Referring to the close link between lack of water and women's desperate lives in the Thar Desert, Grey writes:

This minimal supply of water defines the contours of the day. It means that the little amount of water for washing goes to their menfolk, with consequences for their own hygiene and that of their children, who are constantly suffering from water-related diseases. It influences whether there is water for cooking and any for animals – those that have not been turned loose to wander and perish. In the crushing burden of the work of the Rajasthani woman the worst element is the constant anxiety about water.[24]

Both Atkinson and Grey appeal to a Christian creation theology as inspiration for a renewing of the despoliated planet. This theology is further enhanced in the New Testament's picture of redemption through the death and resurrection of Christ, a redemption that embraces the created order. Linking this promise of reconciliation, renewal and replenishment to the plight of women worldwide, huge numbers desperate for water, Grey summarizes her vision:

Longing for water, longing for life and longing for God come together in a resting place where desires are satisfied and fulfilled in justice for vulnerable communities and the earth's own econ-omy. This is our yearning, our hope: that the earth's wounded-ness will be over and together we shall know each other in a flowing world where our yearnings are realized in trust, peace and love. Only then will we awaken to a deeper yearning, and know ourselves held and cherished by the desire of God.[25]

The way ahead

We have seen in this pathway of social change the centrality of liberation theologies – feminist, intercultural, socio-political and ecological – and noted the centrality of the metaphor of prophet. We have instanced the prophetic voices of people such as Vimla, Sophie, Sunita, Tina Hodgett and Mary Grey.

Let us take Vimla as an example of the call to be a prophet. Her feisty campaigning spirit was not afraid to beard the bureaucratic lion in its den, to take up a strongly argued minority position where the underprivileged are being leaned on, and in her determination to find practical solutions for needy people to adopt what Brueggemann calls 'the prophetic imagination',[26] in one case daringly promising a homeless traveller that her newly acquired, empty council house would be filled with furniture by nightfall. Through frantic phone calls, a borrowed van and the generosity of a local church, it was!

And yet in discussion with Vimla some time later, she pointed out to me that few of her fellow workers had retained their 'campaigning edge', often losing their initial prophetic voice and feeling 'corrupted and compromised' by an unyielding socio-political system. Caught between prophetic idealism and a necessitous pragmatism, is there an alternative and complementary metaphor for the likes of Vimla, Sophie and their 'fellow women'? It is in the biblical notion of the **wise one** that we began to see the answer.

The way of wisdom

We saw in Chapter 1 the value of Elaine Graham's 'transformative Christian practice',[27] with its bid for a 'practical wisdom' in the stories of women's experiences and the accounts of other marginalized groups. Such wisdom is ancient and honoured in the pages of Scripture. Personified as a woman, wisdom is woven into the very fabric of the created order:

> When he established the heavens, I [wisdom] was there . . . when he marked out the foundations of the earth, then I was beside him, like a master worker; and I was daily his delight, rejoicing before him always, rejoicing in his inhabited world and delighting in the human race. (Prov. 8.27–31)

Here is a wisdom that delights the heart of God and, in turn, delights in our God-given humanity. However, the voice of wisdom is not some ethereal sound that is divorced from the everyday lives of a needy world. Hers is a voice that is heard in the market place. She 'cries out in the street; in the squares she raises her voice. At the busiest corner she cries out; at the entrance of the city gates she speaks' (Prov. 1.20–21). Here is a cry that echoes in supermarkets, on crowded trains, in the stock exchange and at the football stadium. This voice, though, is largely unheeded. In our modern world, as Martyn Percy puts it, 'Knowledge replaces wisdom; social network sites replace real relationships; technology drives out humanity.'[28] And yet, where wisdom is listened to, there is the beginning of an understanding of 'the fear of the LORD' (Prov. 2.5).

Abigail, the wife of the well-to-do Nabal, was a wise woman. Hearing of her husband's surly and mean treatment of David's followers, who had been diligently protecting Nabal's livestock and herdsmen, she assembled enough food for an army and rode to meet Israel's future king with her peace offering. David, having resolved to wreak vengeance on Nabal's household, praised her for her 'good judgment' (1 Sam. 25.33, NIV) in saving him from bloodshed and a heavy conscience, accepting her generous provisions. In the meantime, Nabal was gorging himself with food and drink; the next morning, on hearing Abigail's account of her meeting with David, he had a heart attack, finally succumbing some ten days later, when 'the LORD struck Nabal and he died' (25.38, NIV).

Here is a living parable of the nature of wisdom and folly, two opposing ways through life, wherein 'Fools think their own way is right, but the wise listen to advice' (Prov. 12.15). Behind the choice of pathway lies the essence of what a person is really like: Abigail was known as 'a woman of good understanding' (1 Sam. 25.3, AV), and Nabal had presumably earned his nickname of 'Fool' (25.25). As Waldemar Janzen points out, 'Wisdom and foolishness are seen as dimensions of *character* more than labels of individual actions.'[29]

Although Abigail is representative of the common people's wisdom, there was clearly also a calling for 'certain well-defined ranks among those wise who stood in the king's service'.[30] It is likely, according to Janzen, that specially trained scribes in both the royal court and the temple were responsible for the literary production of such works as the book of Proverbs and also for infusing the legacy of wisdom with 'insights from their own courtly tradition with its strong international flavor'.[31] That boundary-crossing perspective, with its 'expertise in politics and law',[32] became necessitous in the exilic and post-exilic periods, as Ronald E. Clements reflects:

It is when we pause to think in terms of a situation in which Israel was no longer a nation [with its temple destroyed and kingship and land lost] that we realize how important it was that concepts of morality and social order should have foundations that stretched beyond the boundaries of nationhood. This is why wisdom became such an important aspect of Israel's intellectual and cultural heritage in the post-exilic age.[33]

Thus God's people learned the universality of God-given social, political and moral instructions whose roots, as we have seen, lay in the very creation of the cosmos. It is this sense of the way things are in the world at large – often imponderable, seemingly perverse at times, yet responding to the mandate, 'The fear of the LORD is the beginning of wisdom' (Prov. 9.10) – that is the mainstay of the canonical wisdom literature of Job, Proverbs and Ecclesiastes. Brueggemann takes this universalizing perspective within which to explore 'an alternative model for ministry'[34] in today's culture. In contrast to the confrontational, visionary role of the prophet, with its quest for justice, Brueggemann puts forward the role of the wise one as an advisory and supportive ministry that seeks out wisdom. The call of the wise is as a 'second-string' operative who is self-effacing in his or her support of the power base, be it personal, organizational or institutional. It is a '"ministry at the margin" of the faith community', not given to sermonizing or proclamation but, rather, tackling 'questions of value and reality [that] are wide open and unsettled'.[35] Above all:

What it has going for it comes from below, not from above. It relies only on the power to penetrate, the capacity to discern, the shrewdness to see clearly and deeply when others do not. Thus it has no authority than a functional one; no appeal beyond the authenticity of its insight.[36]

And this brings us full circle, to my conversation with Vimla. We could see the value of the prophetic spirit and bemoaned the loss of its fire when campaigning zeal gave way to the routine decisions of organizational life. But this is where there is hope, I believe, for the way ahead in the Christian struggle for liberation. It is in the dovetailing of the prophetic call with the call of the wise that boundaries of class, wealth, health, gender, age, race and environment can be most effectively crossed. It is here, as the prophet's 'ministry of insight', which is 'from above', can enmesh with that of the wise 'from below', that both God's word and the people's voice can come together. It is where the idealism of the prophet can give way to the pragmatism of wise women and men that the Claires, Sunitas and Justins of this world can experience constructive social change and the wider communities they represent can begin to realize profound socio-political reformation.

Our fifth and final pathway, then, is to be marked by the everyday call of wisdom, a wisdom that is God-given, teachable and a bringer of peace to a troubled world, to individuals, families, networks, institutions and political power bases alike. As the letter of James puts it:

> the wisdom from above is first pure, then peaceable, gentle, willing to yield, full of mercy and good fruits, without a trace of partiality or hypocrisy. And a harvest of righteousness is sown in peace for those who make peace.   (James 3.17–18)

7

Five pathways, one hope

For in hope we were saved. Now hope that is seen is not hope.
For who hopes for what is seen? But if we hope for what we do
not see, we wait for it with patience.   (Romans 8.24–25)

Tina, the pioneer team vicar we met in the last chapter, shared with
me some of her thoughts concerning God's call to the local community. In her ministry, she seeks to avoid 'the Hungry Church
Monster' that could 'eat up' all her available time and draw her back
'into the jaws of the church building, when there are all those people
and situations outside the church where God is working and needs
co-workers to signpost his activity in the world'. She has reflected
on the parable of the sower and offers a fresh perspective on this
well-known narrative:

> When Jesus told the story of the sower who went out to sow,
> he seemed to assume the sower would just start sowing seed on
> the land in its current condition. Perhaps this was in the days
> before fertilizer, compost, and the rest of the products we buy
> to prepare soil for optimum harvest . . . Some years ago a friend
> of mine took up the challenge of 'Ground-Force-ing' my small
> garden. I'm not a gardener, and I was dumbfounded at the
> amount of time she insisted we spend preparing the soil for
> planting. We dug up the soil, removing every foreign inanimate
> object in it. Mainly we took out bits of concrete, brick, and other
> forms of builders' rubble that had been dumped and buried by
> previous generations. We aerated the soil, hoeing like mad-
> women, and then ploughed sacks of compost in till the earth
> changed colour, became dark, peaty and moist. Only then would
> she allow me to put anything into the ground that would grow.[1]

For Tina, God's call to Portishead entails a prolonged period of digging,
removing obstacles to growth and enriching the soil of a fragmented

community. She firmly believes that all this is to be a work of God's Spirit, and initially spent much time sitting in 'lots of parks and other community spaces and imagined scenes taking place there, and asked God what he wanted' her to do. This is a 'time of preparation and patient hard work with no expectation of return'. However, we saw in the last chapter how this period of waiting and praying began to show signs of God-given growth in the community's soil: the link between the local church and Transition Portishead, with their mutual commitment to low-carbon ecology, and the fostering of good relationships and friendships with immigrant women through the children's centre, English classes and the pairing up of 'language partners' with church members.

Here, in Tina's calling, there are signs of the creativity, empathy and imaginative endeavour that typify Daniel H. Pink's 'conceptual era'. Pink, in his bestselling book *A Whole New Mind*, puts forward the observation of four main sequential ages in the past few centuries of humankind's story:

- the agricultural age, up to and including the eighteenth century: the world of agricultural labourers and farmers;
- the industrial age of the nineteenth and first part of the twentieth centuries: the world of factory workers and miners;
- the information age of the last part of the twentieth century: the world of knowledge workers;
- the conceptual age of the twenty-first century: the world of creators and empathizers.[2]

Following the work of Roger W. Sperry, Pink postulates that the 'information age' is characterized by what he calls 'L-Directed Thinking', whereas the 'conceptual age' is marked by 'R-Directed Thinking'.

In the 1950s Sperry investigated epileptic patients in whom the connection between the brain's two hemispheres had been severed on medical grounds, finding a range of distinctive functions depending on which side of the brain was being used. The left hemisphere controls our sense of sequential time and is the centre that enables logic, analysis and abstract thinking; the right hemisphere is concerned with immediacy and operates at the level of intuition, synthesis and imaginative reasoning. Both hemispheres are needed, of course, but, Pink argues, the information age is primarily 'L-Directed', being the era of accountants, lawyers, computer experts and analytical thinkers, while the conceptual age is essentially 'R-Directed', being the world of artists, poets, creative writers and imaginative thinkers. For Pink: 'The left focuses on categories, the right on relationships. The left can grasp the details. But only the right hemisphere can see the big picture.'[3]

Throughout this book we have had glimpses of left and right brain activity. We saw in biblical counselling an example of 'left-brain' thinking, with the essentially analytical, 'cause-and-effect' approach of the 'Bible-only' methodologies and their emphasis on cognition and behaviour and huge commitment to the precise detail of the biblical text. In contrast, we witnessed the development of post-evangelicalism, progressive orthodoxy and Robert Webber's 'younger evangelicals', wherein we found the 'right-brain' mindset with its greater openness to symbol, metaphor and the world of imagination and storytelling. We saw a similar movement in the transition from pastoral counselling's liberalism and its individualism to a post-liberalism that celebrates community, the biblical narrative and an understanding of the symbolism of language.

Let us, in this final chapter, consider some of the developments in the present 'conceptual age' for our pathways to wholeness. We look at new theology, new friendship and, in conclusion, new hope.

New theology

We have already noted the movements towards post-evangelicalism and post-liberalism. Another theological approach of the 'conceptual age' is that of **radical orthodoxy**, acknowledged as a 'Cambridge movement' and pioneered by John Milbank, Catherine Pickstock and Graham Ward. In his *Introducing Radical Orthodoxy*, James K. A. Smith argues that radical orthodoxy is 'orthodox insofar as it seeks to be unapologetically confessional and Christian' and is 'radical insofar as it seeks to critically retrieve premodern roots (*radix*)'. In its retrieval of 'premodern roots' it especially values the insights of the early Church Fathers. As Smith puts it, radical orthodoxy is 'a movement that is so contemporary [that it] is nevertheless deeply committed to tradition, convinced that the insights of the Spirit given to the early church have much to say to the contemporary church – and to the world'.[4]

Another theological approach that is deeply committed to a traditional, confessional, Christian understanding is that of Sarah Coakley, Norris-Hulse Professor of Divinity at the University of Cambridge, who reflects on the hotly debated issue of gender in the light of a Trinitarian theology.

Gender and the Trinity

I mentioned earlier in the book my involvement with Fulcrum, an online site that offers debate in seeking the renewal of the 'evangelical centre'. Unsurprisingly, issues of gender frequently arise and are hotly contested. And, of course, lurking in the undergrowth of differing opinions is the matter of same-sex orientation, a topic that has at times swamped discussion so thoroughly that Fulcrum's leadership felt the need to put a moratorium on the issue for a period. Broadly, the divisiveness rests between those who see the Bible as quite explicitly condemning homosexual sexual relationships for all time and in all circumstances, and others who see the interpretation of the classic 'anti-gay' texts as a matter of understanding the contexts of Old Testament patriarchal laws and New Testament exploitation of slaves and minors.[5] Engaging in this debate sometimes feels like a fly must feel heading straight for a spider's web.

Sarah Coakley addresses the vexed disputes about gender in contemporary society through a **contemplative theology**. She sees that issues of gender matter intensely in our secular culture where humanity is sliced 'normatively into *two* (and only two)', leading to the oppression of 'those who do not fit the binary alternatives',[6] such as gays, lesbians, bisexuals and transsexuals. She also notes that such matters deeply concern 'biblical fundamentalists and conservatives', with their preoccupation with the 'anti-gay' texts and female-to-male subordination.

Over against these two approaches, Coakley offers a third way that, while still taking seriously biblical teaching, emphasizes that 'gender matters because it is about *differentiated, embodied relationship*': first to God, 'but also, and from there, to others'.[7] The meaning of gender is thus profoundly linked with being made 'in God's image'.

It is here that she points towards the need for silent contemplation. At a simple everyday level, Coakley tells how once a week she goes to Westcott House in Cambridge to share silence with a group of ordinands for an hour. She feels that her presence there is saying: 'Silence is more important than anything else. If you put this first, you will then know which emails not to answer, which door-bells not to answer, and the bits of your life will fall into the right order and the bits that don't matter will fall out.'[8] We might say that what is useful for sorting emails is also helpful in sorting males and females!

However, this redemptive path of devotional silence, which embraces human longings and the realities of gender, is not an easy one. As she puts it:

> The very act of contemplation – repeated, lived, embodied, suf-fered – is an act that, by grace and over time, precisely inculcates mental patterns of unmastery, welcomes the dark realms of the unconscious, opens up a radical attention to the other, and instigates an acute awareness of the messy entanglements of sexual desires and desire for God.[9]

And it is this 'messy entanglement', she argues, that can begin to be disentangled through a contemplation that learns to be open before a loving and transformative Triune God. This Christian contemplation, with its 'bodily practice of dispossession, humility and effacement . . . in the Spirit, causes us to learn incarnationally, and only so, the royal way of the Son to the Father'.[10]

Thus Coakley does not offer simple answers to the complex ques-tions that surround gender and sexuality; rather she seeks to redefine the way forward in terms of our need to learn that God, Father, Son and Holy Spirit, mysteriously and wondrously, desires *us* and seeks to purify and transform our desire for him and, through him, for others. As we saw in Chapter 5, contemplative prayer can be described as a 'looking and loving', in the words of Christopher Bryant. For Coakley, this is also a 'looking and being looked at; looking and being loved'. It is through this practical discipline that our sexual longings and our desires for intimacy, whatever our inherent gender, are set in order, purified and transformed.

New friendship

Throughout this book we have explored a specifically Christian approach to pastoral care and pathways to wholeness. What might other faith traditions have to say about the call to care for those in need, and what might Christian pastoral carers and counsellors learn from such? In *Fear and Friendship*, Sarah Coakley introduces a study of 'Anglicans engaging with Islam' that explores a range of encounters between Christians and Muslims, which in turn lead 'from fear to friendship'. She cites a number of stories that illustrate this venture:

> Often in these narratives, we find the most unexpected and counterintuitive twists and turns: the evangelical Mission church in Birmingham which ended up building a large day centre for its Muslim neighbours in Springfield with absolutely no interest in converting them; the Saudi student who set out to harangue or convert his local parish priest but in fact inspired him to say his own daily office *outside* his church building, as a quiet public witness of fidelity to the broken-down neighbourhood they both shared; the cathedral canon who hit on the extraordinary spiritual creativity of discussing inter-religious tensions with a group of Muslim women via the medium of a Shakespeare play . . .[11]

One outstanding example of such adventurous engagements is that of scriptural reasoning.

Scriptural reasoning

At the end of the last chapter we explored the 'way of wisdom' in relation to the need for social transformation. David F. Ford, Emeritus Professor of Divinity at the University of Cambridge, describes scriptural reasoning as 'a wisdom-seeking engagement with Jewish, Christian and Muslim scriptures' that offers 'a possible contribution to the public sphere in the twenty-first century'.[12]

Ford shows how scriptural reasoning was shaped by its precursor, textual reasoning, in which scholarly Jews in the early 1990s in the United States met to study and interpret the texts of Scripture and the Talmud, especially in the light of post-Shoah Judaism. Christian academics soon joined these gatherings, and shortly afterwards 'scriptural reasoning' was established in Cambridge under the aegis of David Ford and others, initially between Jews and Christians and then, in the late 1990s, between Jews, Christians and Muslims. Of this venture, Ford writes:

A recurring image used to describe the social dynamics of this encounter is that of hospitality – and the resources of each scripture on hospitality have often been a focus for study. Yet this is three-way mutual hospitality: each is host to the others and guest of the others as each welcomes the other two to their 'home' scripture and its traditions of interpretation. As in any form of hospitality, joint study is helped by observing certain customs and guidelines that have been developed through experience over time.[13]

Ford lists these guidelines as follows:

- Acknowledge the sacredness of the others' Scriptures.
- Admit that speakers from each faith tradition do not exclusively own their Scriptures.
- Avoid comforting consensus but, rather, recognize deep differences.
- Do not fear argument, but seek to argue in courtesy and in truth.
- Draw on shared academic resources.
- Allow time to read and re-read the Scripture studied.
- Read and interpret with the aim of fulfilling God's purpose of peace between all.
- Be open to mutual hospitality turning into friendship.[14]

Although Ford engages with scriptural reasoning in an academic context, this practice of mutual hospitality has also sprung up in more everyday settings. For example, Catriona Laing has experience of scriptural reasoning both in the university setting of Cambridge and in a Muslim–Christian group in the city of Bradford. She gives an example in which Mounira presents the Muslim text from the Qur'an, Sura 17:23–24, which includes the phrase, 'Thy Lord hath decreed that ye worship none but Him, and that ye be kind to parents.' In the following discussion, Keith introduces the Christian text from Ephesians 6.4 (NIV): 'Fathers, do not exasperate your children; instead, bring them up in the training and instruction of the Lord.' Laing picks up the conversation as Pippa joins in:

> I rejoin the conversation as Pippa is using the text to probe the topic of parenting a little further. 'It's interesting that the Qur'anic passages look at how children should treat

their parents where the Biblical ones consider how parents should treat their children.' Usama nods in agreement: 'We have this growing problem in the Muslim community where parents are not thinking about what is best for their child, they are taking away the right of the child to choose – for example, who they marry. The way this passage emphasizes the rights of the child is helpful. British Muslims need to think about this.' At this moment our scriptural world is edging into our lived world as we consider what resources for living well together in Bradford might be found in our scriptures.[15]

In such courteous and truth-seeking discussion we see, once more, the creative and imaginative reasoning of the 'conceptual age', an engagement that moves from fear to friendship, from the unknown to the increasingly known. Such encounters can bring new hope to individuals and communities.

New hope

Throughout this book we have glimpsed the aspirations and desires of individuals and groups for a new hope, for new beginnings, new understandings and a sense of breaking new ground on life's journey. We have seen in biblical counselling the quest for a transformed mind, leading to changed behaviour; in the healing and sustaining ministries the forward gain of a new sense of wholeness; in pastoral counselling the longing for a psychological maturity marked by interdependence; in spiritual direction a desire for an uncomplicated heart that responds to a desiring God; and in social change brave attempts to shape a reformed community through hearing the voices of women, the dispossessed and a created order despoiled by human greed and neglect.

These five pathways to wholeness offer, however inadequately at times, routes through life in a troubled world that are bringers of hope. In the often cynical mindsets of our modern and post-modern social environment, 'hope' is seen as a very meagre word. We say, 'I hope so,' often in a wistful and self-defeating manner; 'there's no harm in hoping,' implying the pointlessness of an enterprise; and 'let's hope for the best,' when with some shoulder shrugging we really have very little expectation of a positive outcome.

Sometimes, too, hope is difficult to hold on to. We feel overwhelmed by circumstances and courage fails. An episode in A. A. Milne's *Winnie-the-Pooh* gently illustrates a loss of nerve:

> 'Piglet,' said Rabbit, taking out a pencil, and licking the end of it, 'you haven't any pluck.' 'It is hard to be brave,' said Piglet, sniffing slightly, 'when you're only a Very Small Animal.'[16]

At times, I felt like a 'Very Small Animal' as I faced the prospect of a quadruple bypass. As a long-standing diabetic, I knew that there were particular risks of a severe stroke, post-operative infection or kidney failure. When, following hospital admission, I was told by the cardiac consultant that I must be operated on 'within the week', I said, 'I'd much rather have an aspirin a day instead!' On the eve of surgery, after being shown the intensive care unit with Joy by a friendly ward sister, I wept. As I wrote in my journal, 'Some Heartfelt Reflections', a little later:

> My anticipatory fear (one of so many) had been 'coming round' in that state of ultimate immobility – unable to move, unable to swallow, unable to function at the most fundamental level (how independent is the amoeba?), including breathing... Instead, there was a twilight zone of peace, of the rhythmic, strangely reassuring, respiratory movements of the 'lung machine' – a sense of a safe(ish!) place to be, a sense of being surrounded by the enveloping arms of family and friends, all enfolded by our loving God.

Here, fear was nudging into a sense of peace and a stirring of hope. In fact, on reflection, hope had been struggling to surface following hospital admission and the week-long wait for surgery. At an immediate and sensory level, there was a picture that our daughter Rache had painted for me, of a tunnel whose traditional darkness was bathed in rainbow colours, with a pool of blood-red, which seemed to symbolize the cross of Christ, merging with the blazing gold of anticipated glory. Joy had shared a similar hope-giving picture of a tunnel that finally opened out on to our patio, where she and I were seated contentedly. At a more reflective and metaphorical level, I remember sharing with my sister Anne, a couple of days before the bypass, the imagery of Christ's crucifixion representing in some way the experience of surgery; his time in the tomb speaking of my drop into the night of anaesthesia; and his rising again symbolic of the aftermath of surgery – either to the challenge of a second-birth experience of learning to breathe once more after 59 years of practice, or to the dawning of Paradise. As I emerged from drugged sleep to the susurrations of medical technology, my first thought was, 'No! I'm pretty sure heaven doesn't have all these digital bleeps, flashing lights and spaghetti-junction of tubing!'

And so whatever our struggles on our pathways to wholeness, what new hope might we reach for as we seek impetus and encouragement? I suggest that there are three aspects to this fresh hopefulness within the Christian tradition: a new essence, a new shaping, and a new heaven and earth.

New essence

Here we find a new identity that is offered us both individually and corporately. A classic statement that supports this is that of 2 Corinthians 5.17: 'So if anyone is in Christ, there is a new creation: everything old has passed away; see, everything has become new!' We have seen this gift of a new essence repeatedly in our fivefold pathways to wholeness: in a transformed mind in Christ; in the forward gain of healing; maturing in Christ, both psychologically and spiritually; and in God-given social change. Tom Wright, in *Surprised by Hope*, argues that such a new identity 'avoids from the start any suggestion that the main or central thing that has happened is that the new Christian has entered a private relationship with God or with Jesus and that this relationship is the main or only thing that matters'. This is not a privatized, individualized 'actualization' in Christ. It is, rather, that the 'new convert knows from the start that he or she is part of God's kingdom-project, which stretches out beyond "me and my salvation" to embrace, or rather to be embraced by, God's worldwide purposes'.[17] Here, 'everything has become new' in God's 'here and now' kingdom and this newness is to be expressed in our engagement with the needs of women and girls, wherever they are oppressed, with bringing justice into the two-thirds world, as through fair trade, and in our commitment to valuing and protecting God's good earth.

New shaping

Although there is a givenness about this new essence, there is still a journey to engage with. There is process as well as a new status. In this new shaping, the cross and resurrection of Christ make possible a dying and rising again in the life of the Church, at both the corporate and the individual level. As Philippians 3.10–11 puts it: 'I want to know Christ and the power of his resurrection and the sharing of his sufferings by becoming like him in his death, if somehow I may attain the resurrection from the dead.'

I have often pondered what it means to 'become like him'. When you think of the remarkable individuality of Christ-like people – St Paul, St Francis of Assisi, St Teresa of Avila, Martin Luther, Dietrich Bonhoeffer, Mother Teresa – you realize that, in spite of their many faults, they show particular aspects of being like their Lord. I have sometimes considered the medieval rose window, like the one in Chartres Cathedral that dates from the late twelfth century, as a metaphor for Christ. In this notion, he is the complete rose window in all its transmitted glory and we, in our growing Christ-likeness, are the individual panes of coloured glass and the tracery that make up the many-petalled rose.

And this new shaping, as we saw in Martyn Percy's 'ecclesial canopy', is not only a moulding of our lives into Christ-likeness but is also a transformative engagement with the societal and political spheres. Luke Bretherton, in his *Christianity and Contemporary Politics*, looks to Jeremiah 29 as a template for political involvement within whatever community we are set in. For the Israelites in exile in Babylon, 'the LORD of hosts' says, 'seek the welfare of the city where I have sent you into exile, and pray to the LORD on its behalf, for in its welfare you will find your welfare' (29.7). Concerning this communal aspect of new shaping, Bretherton likens the plight of the Israelites in exile to the Church today:

> the church no longer has priority and Christians are not in control. The salience of Jeremiah 29 is its call to become part of the public life of the city and to reject the false prophets who perpetuate illusions of escape into a private world of gated communities, religious fantasies centered on Christ's immanent return, or daydreams of revolution; while, at the same time,

Jeremiah wants us not [to] give way to a despairing fatalism that believes nothing will ever change.[18]

New heaven and new earth

The Church's new identity, its identification with Christ's death and rising again, and its new transformative journey in hope, are ultimately to be realized in a new heaven and new earth. As in Proverbs 8, the Wisdom that delights in humanity and the whole created order is to witness creation's setting 'free from its bondage to decay' and its obtaining 'the freedom of the glory of the children of God' (Rom. 8.21). This new heaven and new earth will be marked positively with the loving companionship of a God who is 'at home' with his people, and negatively by the banishment of death, mourning, crying and pain (Rev. 21.1–4).

And for this advent of a new creation, Paul uses the imagery of birth pangs, 'groaning in labour pains until now' (Rom. 8.22). For Wright, 'The very metaphor which Paul chooses for the decisive moment in his argument shows that what he has in mind is not the unmaking of creation, nor simply its steady development, but the drastic and dramatic birth of new creation from the womb of the old.'[19]

This one hope for all things new is not an invitation to the sort of escapism that can be seen in right-wing fundamentalism such as that among some North American Christians, a sitting loose to the wasting of the created order in its concentration on 'the hereafter', but rather a call to engage creatively and obediently to bring in God's kingdom here and now. Here is a call to value God's earth, to paint, write poetry, make music, tend gardens, work to relieve the oppressed, pray, worship and love God and neighbour. And the links between the old order and the new heaven and earth, between our five pathways and our one hope, can only be conjectured. In the words of Tom Wright:

> I don't know what musical instruments we shall have to play Bach in God's new world, though I'm sure Bach's music will be there. I don't know how my planting a tree today will relate to the wonderful trees that there will be in God's recreated world . . . I do not know how the painting an artist paints today in prayer and wisdom will find a place in God's new world. I don't know how our work for the poor, for remission of global

debts, will reappear in that world. But I know that God's new world of justice and joy, of hope for the whole earth, was launched when Jesus came out of the tomb on Easter morning; and I know that he calls his followers to live in him and by the power of his spirit, and so to be new-creation people here and now, bringing signs and symbols of the kingdom to birth on earth and in heaven.[20]

Notes

Foreword: mind the gap

1 Niall Williams, *As It Is in Heaven* (London: Penguin, 1999), p. 64.
2 I owe these thoughts to Richard Holloway, in an unpublished address by him.
3 These are the closing words of a short fragment carved on Raymond Carver's tombstone, Ocean View cemetery, Port Angeles.

1 The journey charted

1 David W. Augsburger, *Pastoral Counseling Across Cultures* (Philadelphia: Westminster Press, 1986), p. 22.
2 Herbert Anderson, 'The Bible and pastoral care', in Paul H. Ballard and Stephen R. Holmes, *The Bible in Pastoral Practice: Readings in the Place and Function of Scripture in the Church* (London: Darton, Longman and Todd, 2005), p. 207.
3 Throughout the book people's names, where appropriate, have been altered, along with other distinguishing features, to preserve anonymity.
4 Leanne Payne, *The Healing Presence* (Eastbourne: Kingsway, 1990), p. 132.
5 Jacob Firet, *Dynamics of Pastoring* (Grand Rapids, MI: Eerdmans, 1986), p. 68.
6 Firet, *Dynamics of Pastoring*, p. 82.
7 The roots of our continuing use of the term 'pastoral' care lie, of course, in the 'pivotal analogy', to use Thomas Oden's words, of the biblical connotation of the shepherd. See Thomas C. Oden, *Pastoral Theology: Essentials of Ministry* (Harper and Row, 1983), pp. 49–63.
8 See, for example, Stephen Pattison, *A Critique of Pastoral Care* (2nd edn, London: SCM Press, 1993), pp. 11–13, where Pattison offers useful criticisms of Clebsch and Jaekle's definition and puts forward his own tentative version: 'pastoral care is that activity, undertaken especially by representative Christian persons, directed towards the elimination and relief of sin and sorrow and the presentation of all people perfect in Christ to God'.
9 William A. Clebsch and Charles R. Jaekle, *Pastoral Care in Historical Perspective* (New York: Jason Aronson, 1975), p. 4.
10 Seward Hiltner, *Preface to Pastoral Theology* (Nashville, TN: Abingdon Press, 1958), pp. 89–172, gives healing, sustaining and guiding as 'the

three aspects of the shepherding perspective' (p. 146). Clebsch and Jaekle acknowledge their debt to this source, while declaring they have developed their 'own meanings for these terms'; see Clebsch and Jaekle, *Pastoral Care.*

11 Clebsch and Jaekle, *Pastoral Care.*

12 David Lyall, *Integrity of Pastoral Care* (London: SPCK, 2001), p. 12.

13 Gordon Lynch, *Pastoral Care and Counselling* (London: Sage, 2002), p. 10.

14 Walter Brueggemann, *Genesis* (Atlanta, GA: John Knox Press, 1982), p. 48.

15 David Tracy, 'The foundations of practical theology', in D. S. Browning (ed.), *Practical Theology: The Emerging Field in Theology, Church, and World* (San Francisco: Harper and Row, 1983), p. 61.

16 David Tracy, *Blessed Rage for Order: The New Pluralism in Theology* (New York: Seabury Press, 1975), p. 243.

17 James Woodward and Stephen Pattison (eds), *The Blackwell Reader in Pastoral and Practical Theology* (Oxford: Blackwell, 2000), p. 7.

18 The American pastoral theologian Seward Hiltner refers to C. T. Seidel's *Pastoral-Theologie* (1749) as the earliest of innumerable German works that first used the term 'pastoral theology'.

19 For detailed histories of practical and pastoral theology, see Woodward and Pattison, *Blackwell Reader*, pp. 1–19; and Lyall, *Integrity of Pastoral Care*, pp. 22–43. For comprehensive reflection on the nature and methods of practical theology, see Paul H. Ballard and John Pritchard, *Practical Theology in Action* (2nd edn, London: SPCK, 2006).

20 John Dunford, *Practical Suggestions for the Newly Ordained* (London: Burns, Oates and Washbourne, 1930), p. 87.

21 The term 'dynamic psychology' covers those psychological approaches, such as psychoanalysis, that emphasize the 'cause-and-effect' nature of a person's or group's drives and motives.

22 The psychology of religion as an academic discipline was strongly influenced in its earlier years by William James's functionalism and pragmatism. See, for example, Roger Hurding, *Roots and Shoots: A Guide to Counselling and Psychotherapy* (London: Hodder and Stoughton, 1985), pp. 18–19, 42, 211–13.

23 Edward Farley argues that practical theology needs rescuing from its 'clerical paradigm' and makes a plea for a praxis which is 'redemptively pervasive of any and all social, political, and cultural spaces', while retaining its distinctive Christian 'world-transforming' influence; see 'Theology and practice outside the clerical paradigm', in Browning, *Practical Theology*, p. 39.

24 Browning, *Practical Theology*, p. 33.

25 Seward Hiltner, *Preface to Pastoral Theology*, p. 20.

26 Ballard and Pritchard, *Practical Theology in Action*, p. 21.

27 For a thorough exploration of the complexity and flexibility of practical and pastoral theology, see Woodward and Pattison, *Blackwell Reader*.

28 Glenn H. Asquith, 'The case study method of Anton T. Boisen', *Journal of Pastoral Care*, 34/2 (1980), p. 94.

29 Roger Lundin, *The Culture of Interpretation: Christian Faith and the Postmodern World* (Grand Rapids, MI: Eerdmans, 1993), p. 42, where he argues that at the end of the eighteenth century the Enlightenment's rationalism and empiricism gave way to the 'culture of interpretation'.

30 Charles V. Gerkin, *Living Human Documents: Re-Visioning Pastoral Counseling in a Hermeneutical Mode* (Nashville, TN: Abingdon Press, 1984), pp. 138–9.

31 Jürgen Moltmann, in E. Moltmann-Wendel and J. Moltmann, *Humanity in God* (London: SCM Press, 1983), p. 59.

32 Stephen Pattison, *Pastoral Care and Liberation Theology* (London: SPCK, 1997), p. 2.

33 See, for example, Duncan B. Forrester, *Theology and Politics* (Oxford: Blackwell, 1988); Elaine L. Graham, *Transforming Practice: Pastoral Theology in an Age of Uncertainty* (London: Mowbray, 1996); and Pattison, *Pastoral Care and Liberation Theology*.

34 Graham, *Transforming Practice*, p. 140. Graham looks to the Aristotelian notion of practical wisdom (*phronesis*), where values are 'expressed not in abstract knowledge-claims but in the patterns and orderings of purposeful human activity' (p. 7).

35 Graham, *Transforming Practice*, p. 155.

36 Graham, *Transforming Practice*, p. 165, citing Nancy Fraser, 'What's critical about critical theory?', in S. Benhabib and D. Cornell (eds), *Feminism as Critique: Essays on the Politics of Gender in Late Capitalist Societies* (Cambridge: Polity Press, 1987).

37 See, for example, Sandra Laville's report in *The Guardian*, 22 July 2012.

38 Graham, *Transforming Practice*, pp. 164–5.

39 See Ballard and Pritchard, *Practical Theology in Action*, pp. 81–95.

40 Laurie Green, *Let's Do Theology: A Pastoral Cycle Resource Book* (London: Mowbray, 1990), p. 22.

41 Green, *Let's Do Theology*, p. 25. For an overview of Green's 'doing theology spiral', see pp. 24–32, where the spiral of care moves through a sequence of facing life's **experience** (acknowledging initial feelings and reactions), engaging with an **exploration** of the issues, followed by **reflection** to see how the Christian faith and tradition fit the situation and, finally, to **response**, in which those who are 'doing theology' use their new insights to assess a range of ways forward, from resolute action

to a quiet acceptance of the freshly understood issues. Inevitably, in time, fresh experience leads to a **new situation** and a further opening up of the spiral of care.

42 Laurie Green, *Power to the Powerless: Theology Brought to Life* (Basingstoke: Marshall Pickering, 1987), pp. 16–17.

43 Green, *Power to the Powerless*, p. 10.

44 Green, *Power to the Powerless*, p. 39.

45 Green, *Power to the Powerless*, pp. 137–8.

46 See <www.communities.gov.uk/publications/communities/listening troubledfamilies>.

47 Robert Macfarlane, *The Old Ways: A Journey on Foot* (London: Hamish Hamilton, 2012), p. 24.

48 David Kelsey, *Uses of Scripture in Recent Theology* (London: SCM Press, 1975), p. 215.

2 Biblical counselling: the transformed mind

1 Richard F. Lovelace, *Dynamics of Spiritual Life: An Evangelical Theology of Renewal* (Exeter: Paternoster Press, 1979), p. 219.

2 For a fuller account of the Christian responses to the secular psychologies in assimilation, reaction and dialogue, see Roger Hurding, *Roots and Shoots: A Guide to Counselling and Psychotherapy* (London: Hodder and Stoughton, 1985, 2003), pp. 211–42. This book was published in the United States as *The Tree of Healing* (Grand Rapids, MI: Zondervan, 1988).

3 See Jay E. Adams, *Competent to Counsel* (Grand Rapids, MI: Baker Book House, 1970), pp. xiv–xviii, where he describes his reading of O. Hobart Mowrer, *The Crisis in Psychiatry and Religion* (Princeton, NJ: Van Nostrand Company, 1961) as 'an earth-shaking experience' (p. xvi).

4 See Cornelius Van Til, *The Defense of the Faith* (Phillipsburg, NJ: Presbyterian and Reformed, 1955), pp. 286–99, 306.

5 For example: 'Biblically, there is no warrant for acknowledging the existence of a separate and distinct discipline called psychiatry. There are, in the Scriptures, only three specified sources of personal problems in living: demonic activity . . . personal sin, and organic illness'; there is 'no room for a fourth: non-organic mental illness'. See Jay E. Adams, *The Christian Counselor's Manual* (Phillipsburg, NJ: Presbyterian and Reformed, 1973), p. 9.

6 The terms are comparatively rare in the Greek texts: a handful of references in the Septuagint's Wisdom literature and, in the New Testament, *nouthesia* three times and *noutheteo* eight times. These are quintessentially Pauline words; see, for example, Rom. 15.14; 1 Cor. 4.14; 10.11; Col. 1.28; 3.16; and 1 Thess. 5.12, 14.

7 Van Til, *Defense of the Faith*, p. 286.

8 Jay E. Adams, *More Than Redemption: A Theology of Christian Counseling* (Grand Rapids, MI: Baker Book House, 1979), p. 326.

9 Jay E. Adams, 'Nouthetic counseling', in G. R. Collins (ed.), *Helping People Grow: Practical Approaches to Christian Counseling* (Santa Ana, CA: Vision House, 1980), p. 158.

10 For example, there are at least 45 references to the book of Proverbs and just two to Isaiah in Adams, *Competent to Counsel*.

11 Adams, *Competent to Counsel*, p. 51.

12 See, for example, Donald Capps, *Biblical Approaches to Pastoral Counseling* (Philadelphia: Westminster Press, 1981), pp. 32–6, 99–102, 114–17; John D. Carter, 'Adams' theory of nouthetic counseling', *Journal of Psychology and Theology*, 3/3 (1975), pp. 143–55; Hurding, *Roots and Shoots*, pp. 284–90; Stanton L. Jones and Richard E. Butman, *Modern Psychotherapies: A Comprehensive Christian Appraisal* (Downers Grove, IL: InterVarsity Press, 1991), pp. 18–26; and Richard D. Winter, 'Jay Adams – is he really biblical enough?', *Third Way*, 5/4 (1982), pp. 9–12.

13 In a personal meeting with Jay Adams and a small group of Christian counsellors in Hildenborough Hall, Kent, in May 1982, Adams expressed his regret at committing himself so resolutely to the term 'nouthetic'.

14 See David Powlison, 'Contemporary biblical counseling: an annotated bibliography', *Journal of Biblical Counseling*, 12/2 (1994), pp. 43–61; Powlison writes of 'the modern biblical counseling movement founded by Jay Adams in the late 1960s' (p. 43).

15 David Powlison, '25 years of biblical counseling: an interview with Jay Adams and Jon Bettler', *Journal of Biblical Counseling*, 12/1 (1993), pp. 8–13, see pp. 9–11.

16 John F. Bettler, 'Counseling and the problem of the past', *Journal of Biblical Counseling*, 12/2 (1994) pp. 5–23, see p. 7.

17 David Powlison, *The Biblical Counseling Movement: History and Context* (Greensboro, NC: New Grove Press, 2010), p. 145.

18 Powlison, *Biblical Counseling Movement*, pp. 27–8.

19 Powlison, *Biblical Counseling Movement*, p. 28.

20 Lawrence J. Crabb, *Basic Principles of Biblical Counseling* (Grand Rapids, MI: Zondervan, 1975), p. 18.

21 The original impetus for the formation of ABC is closely linked with seminars conducted by Jay Adams in 1981 and 1982, and by his colleagues John Bettler and Wayne Mack in the following years, at Hildenborough Hall, Kent.

22 For a helpful overview of the development of ACC from 1992 to 2012, see 'Looking back on 20 years of ACC', *Accord*, 75, Summer 2012, pp. 19–22.

23 See Powlison, *Biblical Counseling Movement*, pp. 212–13.

24 Martin Bobgan and Deirdre Bobgan, *The Psychological Way/The Spiritual Way* (Ada, MI: Bethany House, 1979), pp. 10–12.

25 See Martin Bobgan and Deirdre Bobgan, *Against 'Biblical Counseling': For the Bible* (Santa Barbara, CA: Eastgate, 1998), pp. 10–14.

26 Bobgan and Bobgan, *Against 'Biblical Counseling'*, p. 167.

27 For books that explore so-called secular psychotherapists in depth and from a Christian perspective, see Hurding, *Roots and Shoots*; L. Stanton Jones and Richard E. Butman, *Modern Psychotherapies: A Comprehensive Christian Appraisal* (Downers Grove, IL: InterVarsity Press, 1991); and Siang-Yang Tan, *Counseling and Psychotherapy: A Christian Perspective* (Grand Rapids, MI: Baker Books, 2011).

28 E. S. Williams, *The Dark Side of Christian Counselling* (London: Wakeman Trust, 2009), p. 85.

29 Williams, *Dark Side of Christian Counselling*, p. 42.

30 Williams, *Dark Side of Christian Counselling*, pp. 32–3.

31 Williams, *Dark Side of Christian Counselling*, pp. 27–9.

32 Williams, *Dark Side of Christian Counselling*, p. 148.

33 See Alister E. McGrath, *A Passion for Truth: The Intellectual Coherence of Evangelicalism* (Leicester: Inter-Varsity Press, 1996), pp. 167–70.

34 McGrath, *A Passion For Truth*, p. 169.

35 Bernard Ramm, *Special Revelation and the Word of God* (Grand Rapids, MI: Eerdmans, 1961), p. 20.

36 McGrath, *A Passion for Truth*, p. 170.

37 David Powlison, 'Critiquing modern integrationists', *Journal of Biblical Counseling*, 11/3 (1993), pp. 30–1.

38 G. C. Berkouwer, *General Revelation* (Grand Rapids, MI: Eerdmans, 1955), p. 162.

39 Arthur F. Holmes, *All Truth is God's Truth* (Grand Rapids, MI: Eerdmans, 1977), p. 8.

40 Robert E. Webber, *The Younger Evangelicals: Facing the Challenges of the New World* (Grand Rapids, MI: Baker Books, 2002), p. 15.

41 For appraisals of pastoral care in relation to postmodernism, see Paul Goodliff, *Care in a Confused Climate: Pastoral Care and Postmodern Culture* (London: Darton, Longman and Todd, 1998), and Roger Hurding, *Pathways to Wholeness: Pastoral Care in a Postmodern Age* (London: Hodder and Stoughton, 1998).

42 Webber, *Younger Evangelicals*, p. 17.

43 Dave Tomlinson, *The Post-Evangelical* (London: SPCK, 1995), p. 90.

3 Healing ministries: the forward gain

1 Ursula Le Guin, *Earthsea Trilogy* (Harmondsworth: Pelican, 1979), p. 165.

2 William A. Clebsch and Charles R. Jaekle, *Pastoral Care in Historical Perspective* (New York: Jason Aronson, 1975), p. 42.

3 It is worth pointing out at this stage that healing, because it is a comprehensive concept, can be seen to feature in all of the five pathways.

4 Morris Maddocks, *The Christian Healing Ministry* (London: SPCK, 1981), p. 7.

5 Clebsch and Jaekle, *Pastoral Care*, p. 33.

6 Clebsch and Jaekle, *Pastoral Care*, p. 8. Books on 'healing' often fail to balance their approach with a consideration of 'sustaining'. Stephen Pattison, *Alive and Kicking: Towards a Practical Theology of Illness and Healing* (London: SCM Press, 1989) is a notable exception.

7 This term is culled from Peter's Pentecostal sermon in which, seeing the Spirit's manifestations in tongues and fire, he declares, 'this is what was spoken through the prophet Joel' (Acts 2.16).

8 See Mark Stibbe, *Times of Refreshing: A Practical Theology of Renewal for Today* (London: HarperCollins, 1995), pp. 3–29. For a detailed refutation of Stibbe's approach, see Mark Smith, '"This-is-that" hermeneutics', in Lloyd Pietersen (ed.), *The Mark of the Spirit? A Charismatic Critique of the Toronto Blessing* (Carlisle: Paternoster Press, 1998).

9 Neil T. Anderson, *Steps to Freedom in Christ* (Oxford and Grand Rapids, MI: Monarch, 2009), p. 30.

10 Anderson, *Steps to Freedom*, pp. 36–9.

11 Anderson, *Steps to Freedom*, p. 10.

12 Anderson, *Steps to Freedom*, p. 10.

13 Elliot Miller, 'Neil Anderson and Freedom in Christ ministries: a general critique', *Christian Research Journal*, 21/1 (1998). The introductory section of this article can be seen at <www.equip.org/articles/neil-anderson-and-freedom-in-christ-ministries-a-general-critique/>.

14 Mark A. Pearson, *Christian Healing: A Practical and Comprehensive Guide* (Lake Mary, FL: Charisma House, 2004), p. 160.

15 Pearson, *Christian Healing*, p. 163.

16 Ruth Carter Stapleton, *The Experience of Inner Healing* (London: Hodder and Stoughton, 1978), Introduction.

17 Agnes Sanford, *Healing Gifts of the Spirit* (Evesham: Arthur James, 1966), pp. 86–7.

18 Sanford, *Healing Gifts*, p. 101.

19 Sanford, *Healing Gifts*, p. 107.

20 Sanford, *Healing Gifts*, p. 95.

21 Dave Hunt and T. A. McMahon, *The Seduction of Christianity: Spiritual Discernment in the Last Days* (Eugene, OR: Harvest House, 1985).

22 Hunt and McMahon, *Seduction of Christianity*, pp. 171–88.

23 Hunt and McMahon, *Seduction of Christianity*, p. 165.

24 Hunt and McMahon, *Seduction of Christianity*, p. 173.

25 Dan B. Allender, *The Healing Path* (Colorado Springs: Waterbrook Press, 1999), p. 184. For helpful approaches to healing of the past, see David G. Benner, *Healing Emotional Wounds* (Grand Rapids, MI: Baker Book House, 1990), and Dan B. Allender, *The Wounded Heart* (Colorado Springs: NavPress, 2008).

26 Roger Hurding, *As Trees Walking* (Exeter: Paternoster Press, 1982), p. 214.

27 For a compassionate appraisal of evil in a pastoral context, see John Swinton, *Raging with Compassion: Pastoral Responses to the Problem of Evil* (Cambridge and Grand Rapids, MI: Eerdmans, 2007).

28 C. S. Lewis, *Screwtape Letters* (London: Collins, 1955), p. 9.

29 Walter Wink, *Naming the Powers: The Language of Power in the New Testament* (Philadelphia: Fortress Press, 1984), p. 4.

30 Wink, *Naming the Powers*, p. x.

31 Wink, *Naming the Powers*, p. 5.

32 Wink, *Naming the Powers*, p. 5.

33 Walter Wink, *Unmasking the Powers: The Invisible Forces that Determine Human Existence* (Philadelphia: Fortress Press, 1986), p. 7.

34 Wink, *Unmasking the Powers*, p. 25.

35 Wink, *Unmasking the Powers*, pp. 9–10.

36 Annie Dillard, *Pilgrim at Tinker Creek* (Norwich: Canterbury Press, 2011), p. 230.

37 Prospects is a voluntary Christian organization that works 'together with people with learning disabilities so they live life to the full'. See <www.prospects.org.uk/>.

38 Mary Grey, 'The spiritual journey of impaired pilgrims', in Donald Eadie *et al.*, *The Faith Journey of Impaired Pilgrims* (Salisbury: Sarum College Press, 2006), p. 6.

39 Henri J. M. Nouwen, *The Wounded Healer* (New York: Doubleday, 1979), pp. 81–96.

40 Mary Grey, 'Devouring mother or wounded healer? Liberating new models of caring in feminist theology', in Otto Stange (ed.), *Pastoral Care and Context* (Amsterdam: VU University Press, 1992), p. 95.

4 Pastoral counselling: the maturing person

1 Paul Tillich, *The Courage To Be* (London: Nisbet, 1952), p. 85.

2 William A. Clebsch and Charles R. Jaekle, *Pastoral Care in Historical Perspective* (New York: Jason Aronson, 1975), p. 4.

3 From the preamble to the AAPC constitution, quoted in Alastair V. Campbell, *Paid to Care? The Limits of Professionalism in Pastoral Care* (London: SPCK, 1985), p. 37.

4 Don S. Browning, 'Introduction to pastoral counseling', in R. J. Wicks, R. D. Parsons and D. E. Capps (eds), *Clinical Handbook of Pastoral Counseling* (New York: Paulist Press, 1985), p. 6; for a discussion of the definitions of pastoral care, pastoral counselling and pastoral psychotherapy, see pp. 5–7.

5 For valuable discussions on the sometimes bewildering range of usages of the term 'pastoral counselling', see David Lyall, *Counselling in the Pastoral and Spiritual Context* (Buckingham: Open University Press, 1995), pp. 36–8; Alistair Ross, 'The future of pastoral counselling', *The Whitefield Institute Briefing*, 1/2 (1996), pp. 1–4; and Peter J. Van de Kasteele, 'Pastoral counselling', *Clinical Theology Association Newsletter*, 67 (1996), pp. 4–5.

6 See, especially, Thomas C. Oden, 'Recovering lost identity', *Journal of Pastoral Care*, 34/1 (1980), pp. 4–18; *Pastoral Theology: Essentials of Ministry* (San Francisco: Harper and Row, 1983); *Pastoral Counsel*, Vol. 3 (New York: Crossroad Publishing, 1989); and 'The historic pastoral care tradition: a resource for Christian psychologists', *Journal of Psychology and Theology*, 20/2 (1992), pp. 137–46.

7 For a fuller account of Weatherhead's and Kyle's contributions to pastoral counselling in Britain, see Roger Hurding, *Roots and Shoots: A Guide to Counselling and Psychotherapy* (London: Hodder and Stoughton, 1985), pp. 216–21, 224–7.

8 David Black, *A Place for Exploration: The Story of the Westminster Pastoral Foundation 1969–1990* (London: Westminster Pastoral Foundation, 1991), pp. 64–5.

9 R. A. Lambourne, 'With love to the USA', *Religion and Medicine* (London: SCM Press, 1970), p. 132, quoted in Lyall, *Counselling*, p. 27.

10 R. A. Lambourne, 'Objections to a national pastoral organisation', *Contact*, 35 (1971), pp. 27–8.

11 Lambourne, 'Objections', pp. 27–8.

12 Lambourne, 'Objections', p. 27.

13 For the continuing debate around Lambourne's thesis, see Campbell, *Paid to Care?*, pp. 37–40; Lyall, *Counselling*, pp. 26–9, 109–10; and Michael Northcott, 'The new age and pastoral theology: towards the resurgence of the sacred', *Contact Pastoral Monograph*, no. 2 (1992), pp. 22–5.

14 Lyall, *Counselling*, p. 28.

15 Among recent papers that urge pastoral counselling towards a greater theological sophistication, see Gordon Lynch, 'Moral reflection and the Christian pastoral counsellor', *Contact*, 117 (1995), pp. 3–8; and 'Where is the theology of British pastoral counselling?', *Contact*, 121 (1996), pp. 22–8. For works that take this injunction seriously, see Francis Bridger and David Atkinson, *Counselling in Context: Developing a Theological Framework* (London: HarperCollins, 1994); and Paul Goodliff,

Care in a Confused Climate: Pastoral Care and Postmodern Culture (London: Darton, Longman and Todd, 1998).

16 Quoted by David L. Edwards, *Church Times*, 29 December 1989, p. 11.

17 Rollo May, *Paulus: A Personal Portrait of Paul Tillich* (London: Collins, 1974), p. 86.

18 May, *Paulus*, p. 87.

19 Tillich, *Courage To Be*, p. 37.

20 Tillich, *Courage To Be*, p. 178.

21 Elaine L. Graham, *Transforming Practice: Pastoral Theology in an Age of Uncertainty* (London: Mowbray, 1996), p. 70.

22 David Tracy puts forward a revision of Tillich's method of correlation. Whereas Tillich's approach is in just one direction, with philosophy asking the questions and theology answering them, for Tracy there is two-way traffic with questions and answers from both sources: from 'Christian texts' and 'common human experience and language'. See David Tracy, *Blessed Rage for Order: The New Pluralism in Theology* (New York: Seabury Press, 1975), p. 46.

23 Alister E. McGrath, *A Passion for Truth: The Intellectual Coherence of Evangelicalsm* (Leicester: Inter-Varsity Press, 1996), pp. 120–61, where he presents a sympathetic evangelical critique of post-liberalism.

24 Emmanuel Y. Lartey, *Pastoral Counselling in Inter-Cultural Perspective* (Frankfurt am Main: Peter Lang, 1987), pp. 25–6.

25 Lartey, *Pastoral Counselling*, p. 68.

26 Lartey, *Pastoral Counselling*, p. 146.

27 Lartey, *Pastoral Counselling*, pp. 146–7, quoting Karl Barth, *Church Dogmatics*, ed. G. W. Bromiley and T. F. Torrance (Edinburgh: T & T Clark, 1961), Vol. 3, Part 4, pp. 199, 203.

28 Clyde Kluckhohn and Henry A. Murray, *Personality in Nature, Society and Culture* (New York: Alfred A. Knopf, 1948), p. 53, quoted in Susan Rakoczy, 'Unity, diversity, and uniqueness: foundations of cross-cultural spiritual direction', in S. Rakoczy (ed.), *Common Journey, Different Paths: Spiritual Direction in Cross-Cultural Perspective* (Maryknoll, NY: Orbis Books, 1992), p. 10.

29 John S. Mbiti, *African Religions and Philosophy* (London: Heinemann Educational, 1969), pp. 108–9, in Rakoczy, *Common Journey*, p. 14.

30 Robert Kegan, *The Evolving Self: Problem and Process in Human Development* (Cambridge, MA: Harvard University Press, 1982), p. 11.

31 Kegan, *Evolving Self*, p. 15.

32 Joann Wolski Conn, *Spirituality and Personal Maturity* (Mahwah, NJ: Paulist Press, 1989), pp. 57–8.

33 C. K. Barrett, quoted in David Prior, *The Message of 1 Corinthians* (Leicester: Inter-Varsity Press, 1985), p. 56.

34 Richard Dawkins, *The Selfish Gene* (London: Oxford University Press, 1976), in which the socio-biologist Dawkins postulates that it is in the survival 'interests' of their genetic make-up that individuals compete successfully and reproduce effectively.

35 Aldous Huxley, 'Visionary experience', in John White (ed.), *The Highest State of Consciousness* (New York: Archer, 1972), quoted in Kegan, *Evolving Self*, p. 11.

36 Kegan, *Evolving Self*, p. 107.

37 Kegan, *Evolving Self*, p. 108. Kegan's is one of many theories of maturation. Perhaps the best known, based on stages of handling the 'meaning of life', is found in James W. Fowler, *Stages of Faith: The Psychology of Human Development and the Quest for Meaning* (San Francisco: HarperCollins, 1995). Nicola Slee, in *Women's Faith Development: Patterns and Processes* (Aldershot: Ashgate, 2004), is affirmative of Fowler's approach yet sees it as to some extent androcentric. She puts forward her enquiry into women's faith journeys by collating the stories of 30 women she interviews.

38 Kegan, *Evolving Self*, pp. 108–9.

39 Kegan, *Evolving Self*, p. 274.

40 Conn, *Spirituality and Personal Maturity*, p. 56.

41 David G. Benner, *Psychotherapy and the Spiritual Quest* (Grand Rapids: Baker Book House, 1988), p. 133: 'psychospiritual maturity is characterized by integration of personality, which occurs within a context of significant interpersonal relationships and surrender to God.' See pp. 104–33 for his full treatment of this perspective.

42 Benner, *Psychotherapy*, p. 57.

43 Alistair Ross, *Counselling Skills for Church and Faith Community Workers* (Maidenhead and Philadelphia: Open University Press, 2003).

44 Thomas C. Oden, *Kerygma and Counseling: Toward a Covenant Ontology for Secular Psychology* (2nd edn, San Francisco: Harper and Row, 1978), p. 9.

45 Oden, *Kerygma and Counseling*, pp. 23–4.

46 Donald Capps, *Biblical Approaches to Pastoral Counseling* (Philadelphia: Westminster Press, 1981), p. 12.

47 Capps, *Biblical Approaches*, p. 59.

48 Walter Brueggemann, 'The formfulness of grief', *Interpretation*, 31/3 (1977), pp. 263–75.

49 Brueggemann, 'Formfulness', p. 267.

50 David F. Ford, *Self and Salvation: Being Transformed* (Cambridge: Cambridge University Press, 1999), p. 104.

5 Spiritual direction: the uncomplicated heart

1 Richard Baxter, 1696, in J. M. L. Thompson (ed.), *The Autobiography* (London: Dent, 1931), p. 7, quoted in Roger Pooley and Philip Seddon

(eds), *The Lord of the Journey: A Reader in Christian Spirituality* (London: Collins, 1986), p. 80.

2 Cited in Morton T. Kelsey, *The Other Side of Silence: A Guide to Christian Meditation* (London: SPCK, 1977), pp. 127–8, dating the remark to Cincinnati in 1941.

3 Evelyn Underhill, *Mysticism: A Study in the Nature and Development of Man's Spiritual Consciousness* (11th edn, London: Methuen, 1926), p. ix. See too Melvyn Matthews, *Awake to God: Explorations in the Mystical Way* (London, SPCK, 2006).

4 Robert E. Webber, *The Divine Embrace: Recovering the Passionate Spiritual Life* (Grand Rapids, MI: Baker Books, 2006), p. 16.

5 Belden C. Lane, *The Solace of Fierce Landscapes: Exploring Desert and Mountain Spirituality* (Oxford and New York: Oxford University Press, 1998), p. 64.

6 Anthony Meredith, *The Cappadocians* (London: Geoffrey Chapman, 1995), p. 59.

7 Andrew Louth, in Gordon S. Wakefield (ed.), *Dictionary of Christian Spirituality* (London: SCM Press, 1983), p. 109.

8 *The Cloud of Unknowing* (6th edn, London: John M. Watkins, 1956), chapter 70, p. 256.

9 Walter Brueggemann, *In Man We Trust: The Neglected Side of Biblical Faith* (Atlanta, GA: John Knox Press, 1972), p. 105.

10 For Waldemar Janzen, 'To live life in constant and zealous attention to Yahweh's holy presence constitutes the first great ethical imperative within the priestly paradigm of the good life'; see Waldemar Janzen, *Old Testament Ethics: A Paradigmatic Approach* (Louisville, KY: Westminster/John Knox, 1994), pp. 106–7. The relevance of this 'priestly paradigm' for the continuing Church tradition of spiritual direction is, I suggest, clear.

11 David Runcorn, *Spirituality Workbook: A Guide for Explorers, Pilgrims and Seekers* (London: SPCK, 2006), p. 10.

12 Louis Bouyer, *Orthodox Spirituality and Protestant and Anglican Spirituality* (*A History of Christian Spirituality*, Vol. 3) (New York: Seabury Press, 1969), p. 47.

13 Christopher Bryant, *The River Within: The Search for God in Depth* (London: Darton, Longman and Todd, 1973), pp. 108–9.

14 See Lane, *Solace of Fierce Landscapes*, p. 12, where he also quotes John Cassian.

15 Kenneth Leech, *Soul Friend: A Study in Spirituality* (London: Sheldon Press, 1986), p. 50.

16 Leech, *Soul Friend*, p. 50.

17 See Margaret Guenther, *Holy Listening: The Art of Spiritual Direction* (London: Darton, Longman and Todd, 1992), pp. 89–106.

18 Tilden Edwards, *Spiritual Friend: Reclaiming the Gift of Spiritual Direction* (New York: Paulist Press, 1980), p. 125.

19 Henri J. M. Nouwen, *Reaching Out: The Three Movements of the Spiritual Life* (Glasgow: Collins, 1976), p. 38.

20 David W. Augsburger, *Pastoral Counseling Across Cultures* (Philadelphia: Westminster Press, 1986), p. 37.

21 David G. Benner, *Psychotherapy and the Spiritual Quest* (Grand Rapids, MI; Baker Book House, 1988), p. 108.

22 See his argument in Benner, *Psychotherapy*, pp. 108–11.

23 Benner, *Psychotherapy*, pp. 114–15, where he follows the argument in A. Wolters, *Creation Regained: Biblical Basics for a Reformational Worldview* (Grand Rapids, MI: Eerdmans, 1985).

24 I am indebted to the writings of Francis Schaeffer (1912–84) for this phrase.

25 See Abraham H. Maslow, *Motivation and Personality* (2nd edn, New York: Harper and Row, 1970), pp. 35–58.

26 Benner, *Psychotherapy*, p. 123.

27 Benner, *Psychotherapy*, p. 123.

28 See Thomas Merton, *Seeds of Contemplation* (2nd edn, Wheathampstead, Herts: Anthony Clarke, 1972).

29 Joann Wolski Conn, *Spirituality and Personal Maturity* (Mahwah, NJ: Paulist Press, 1989), p. 33.

30 Merton, *Seeds of Contemplation*, p. 33.

31 Henri J. M. Nouwen, *Life of the Beloved: Spiritual Living in a Secular World* (London: Hodder and Stoughton, 1993), p. 106.

32 I am particularly indebted to Conn's excellent analysis for much of the thinking in this section; see Conn, *Spirituality and Personal Maturity*, pp. 96–125. See too Peter Madsen Gubi, 'A qualitative exploration of the similarities and differences between counselling and spiritual accompaniment', *Practical Theology*, 4/3 (2011), pp. 339–58.

33 Although the phenomenon of transference is often seen as the prerogative of the psychoanalytic tradition, the transferring of the client's emotions, ideas and attitudes from a significant figure of his or her past to the counsellor can be experienced in any therapeutic approach, including pastoral counselling. Where such relatedness is thus misplaced the counselling process will seek to help the client towards a clarification of the situation, so that in future the true, original object of the client's feelings is discerned constructively.

34 Conn, *Spirituality and Personal Maturity*, p. 96.

35 Martin Thornton, *Spiritual Direction: A Practical Introduction* (London: SPCK, 1984), p. 13.

36 R. A. Lambourne, 'Objections to a national pastoral organisation', *Contact*, 35 (1971), pp. 24–31, see p. 27.

37 Thornton, *Spiritual Direction*, p. 9.

38 Conn, *Spirituality and Personal Maturity*, p. 97.

39 Nicholas Wolterstorff, *Lament for a Son* (London: Hodder and Stoughton, 1989).

40 Conn, *Spirituality and Personal Maturity*, p. 107.

41 Gary W. Moon and David G. Benner (eds), *Spiritual Direction and the Care of Souls: A Guide to Christian Approaches and Practices* (Trowbridge: Eagle, 2004), p. 300.

42 C. S. Lewis, *Till We Have Faces: A Myth Retold* (London: Geoffrey Bles, 1956), p. 104.

43 Lewis, *Till We Have Faces*, p. 189.

44 Lewis, *Till We Have Faces*, p. 305.

45 Lewis, *Till We Have Faces*, p. 319.

46 David F. Ford, *Self and Salvation: Being Transformed* (Cambridge: Cambridge University Press, 1999), p. 172.

47 Ford, *Self and Salvation*, p. 175.

48 Ford, *Self and Salvation*, p. 104.

49 See Annice Callahan (ed.), *Spiritualities of the Heart: Approaches to Personal Wholeness in Christian Tradition* (Mahwah, NJ: Paulist Press, 1990).

50 Merton, *Seeds of Contemplation*, p. 2.

51 Callahan, *Spiritualities of the Heart*, p. 1.

6 Social change: the reformed community

1 Peter Selby, *Liberating God: Private Care and Public Struggle* (London: SPCK, 1983), p. 76.

2 Nicola Slee, *Women's Faith Development: Patterns and Processes* (Aldershot and Burlington, VT: Ashgate, 2004), p. 11.

3 Zoë Bennett Moore, *Introducing Feminist Perspectives on Pastoral Theology* (Sheffield: Sheffield Academic Press, 2002), p. 7.

4 Moore, *Introducing Feminist Perspectives*, p. 12.

5 Moore, *Introducing Feminist Perspectives*, pp. 18–19.

6 Heather Walton, 'Passion and pain: conceiving theology out of infertility', *Contact*, 130 (1999), pp. 7–8.

7 See, for example, her editing of *Searching the Scriptures: A Feminist Introduction* (London: SCM Press, 1994).

8 See Moore, *Introducing Feminist Perspectives*, pp. 56–7 for a helpful overview of Schüssler Fiorenza's approach.

9 Mary Grey, 'Devouring mother or wounded healer? Liberating new models of caring in feminist theology', in Otto Stange (ed.), *Pastoral Care and Context* (Amsterdam: VU University Press, 1992), p. 83.

10 Heather Walton, 'Breaking open the Bible', in E. L. Graham and M. Halsey (eds), *Life Cycles: Women and Pastoral Care* (London: SPCK, 1993), p. 198.

11 Emmanuel Y. Lartey, *In Living Color: An Intercultural Approach to Pastoral Care and Counseling* (London and Philadelphia: Jessica Kingsley, 2003), p. 170. See too Colin Lago and Joyce Thompson, *Race, Culture and Counselling* (Buckingham: Open University Press, 1996).

12 Lartey, *In Living Color*, p. 171, where Lartey cites Clyde Kluckhohn and Henry A. Murray, *Personality in Nature, Society and Culture* (New York: Alfred A. Knopf, 1948).

13 Lartey, *In Living Color*, p. 176.

14 Sallie McFague, *Models of God: Theology for an Ecological, Nuclear Age* (London: SCM Press, 1987), p. 47.

15 Waldemar Janzen, *Old Testament Ethics: A Paradigmatic Approach* (Louisville, KY: Westminster/John Knox, 1994), p. 155.

16 Percy takes the idea of 'the ecclesial canopy' from Peter Berger's 'sacred canopy'.

17 Martyn Percy, *The Ecclesial Canopy: Faith, Hope, Charity* (Aldershot and Burlington, VT: Ashgate, 2012), pp. 1–2. See also Duncan B. Forrester, *Theology and Politics* (Oxford: Blackwell, 1988), and Luke Bretherton with his 'politics of hospitality' in *Christianity and Contemporary Politics* (Chichester and Malden, MA: Wiley-Blackwell, 2010).

18 Percy, *Ecclesial Canopy*, pp. 175–6.

19 See <www.transitionportishead.org.uk/>.

20 See <www.operationnoah.org/>.

21 David Atkinson, *Renewing the Face of the Earth: A Theological and Pastoral Response to Climate Change* (Norwich: Canterbury Press, 2008), p. 18.

22 Mary C. Grey, *Sacred Longings: Ecofeminist Theology and Globalization* (London: SCM Press, 2003), p. 124. See too Sallie McFague, *The Body of God: An Ecological Theology* (London: SCM Press, 1993), where she puts forward a perspective that just as humankind has oppressed the 'old poor' of the underclass, of women and of the culturally different, so humanity, in its greed, rapacity and neglect has oppressed the 'new poor' of the natural order.

23 Grey, *Sacred Longings*, pp. 27–8.

24 Grey, *Sacred Longings*, p. 42.

25 Grey, *Sacred Longings*, pp. 211–12.

26 See, for example, Walter Brueggemann, *Prophetic Imagination* (London: SCM Press, 1978), and *Hopeful Imagination: Prophetic Voices in Exile* (2nd edn, Philadelphia: Fortress Press, 1986).

27 See Elaine Graham, *Transforming Practice: Pastoral Theology in an Age of Uncertainty* (London: Mowbray, 1996), and *Words Made*

Flesh: Writings in Pastoral and Practical Theology (London: SCM Press, 2009).

28 Percy, *Ecclesial Canopy*, p. 184.

29 Janzen, *Old Testament Ethics*, p. 121. For Janzen's assessment of the story of Abigail, Nabal and David, in relation to 'folk wisdom', see pp. 120–2. See too David Runcorn, *Fear and Trust: God-centred Leadership* (London: SPCK, 2011), in which the wisdom of men and women depicted in 1 and 2 Samuel is explored.

30 Janzen, *Old Testament Ethics*, p. 120.

31 Janzen, *Old Testament Ethics*, p. 122.

32 Janzen, *Old Testament Ethics*, p. 164.

33 Ronald E. Clements, *Wisdom for a Changing World: Wisdom in Old Testament Theology* (Berkeley, CA: Bibal Press, 1990), p. 23.

34 Walter Brueggemann, *In Man We Trust: The Neglected Side of Biblical Faith* (Louisville, KY: John Knox Press, 1972), p. 109.

35 Brueggemann, *In Man We Trust*, p. 112.

36 Brueggemann, *In Man We Trust*, p. 111 (italics removed).

7 Five pathways, one hope

1 Used with permission from unpublished material by Tina Hodgett.

2 Daniel H. Pink, *A Whole New Mind: Why Right-Brainers Will Rule the Future* (London and Singapore: Marshall Cavendish, 2008), pp. 48–51. Luke Bretherton is critical of radical orthodoxy for its view that calls into question 'the very possibility of a secular space understood as neutral and uncommitted': *Christianity and Contemporary Politics* (Chichester and Malden, MA: Wiley-Blackwell, 2010), p. 13.

3 Pink, *A Whole New Mind*, p. 23.

4 James K. A. Smith, *Introducing Radical Orthodoxy: Mapping a Post-secular Theology* (Grand Rapids, MI: Baker Academic, 2004), p. 68.

5 Accepting Evangelicals is an open online network 'who believe the time has come to move towards the acceptance of faithful, loving same-sex partnerships at every level of church life, and the development of a positive Christian ethic for lesbian, gay, bisexual and transgender people'. See <www.acceptingevangelicals.org/>.

6 Sarah Coakley, 'Is there a future for gender and theology? On gender, contemplation, and the systematic task', *Criterion*, 47/1 (2009), pp. 2–12, see p. 9. See also her 'God and gender: how theology can find a way through the impasse', on ABC *Religion and Ethics* (8 March 2012) at <www.abc.net.au/religion/articles/2012/03/08/3448940.htm>.

7 Coakley, 'Is there a future', p. 9.

8 Coakley, 'Living Prayer and Leadership' (2009), online at <http://faithandleadership.com/qa/sarah-coakley-living-prayer-and-leadership>.

9 Coakley, 'Is there a future', p. 5.
10 Coakley, 'Is there a future', p. 6.
11 Sarah Coakley, 'Foreword', in Frances Ward and Sarah Coakley (eds), *Fear and Friendship: Anglicans Engaging with Islam* (London and New York: Continuum, 2012), pp. ix–x.
12 David F. Ford, *Christian Wisdom: Desiring God and Learning in Love* (Cambridge: Cambridge University Press, 2007), p. 273.
13 Ford, *Christian Wisdom*, p. 279.
14 Ford, *Christian Wisdom*, pp. 279–80.
15 Catriona Laing, 'Scriptural reasoning', in Ward and Coakley, *Fear and Friendship*, pp. 122–4.
16 A. A. Milne, *Winnie-the-Pooh* (1926), chapter 7.
17 Tom Wright, *Surprised by Hope* (London: SPCK, 2007), pp. 240–1.
18 Bretherton, *Christianity and Contemporary Politics*, p. 5.
19 Wright, *Surprised by Hope*, p. 115.
20 Wright, *Surprised by Hope*, p. 220.

Select bibliography
and further reading

Adams, Jay E., *Competent to Counsel* (Grand Rapids, MI: Baker Book House, 1970).

Adams, Jay E., *The Christian Counselor's Manual* (Phillipsburg, NJ: Presbyterian and Reformed, 1973).

Adams, Jay E., *More Than Redemption: A Theology of Christian Counseling* (Baker Book House, 1979).

Allender, Dan B., *The Healing Path: How the Hurts in Your Past Can Lead You to a More Abundant Life* (Colorado Springs: Waterbrook Press, 1999).

Anderson, Neil T., *Steps to Freedom in Christ* (Oxford and Grand Rapids, MI: Monarch, 2009).

Atkinson, David, *Renewing the Face of the Earth: A Theological and Pastoral Response to Climate Change* (Norwich: Canterbury Press, 2008).

Atkinson, David, *The Church's Healing Ministry: Practical and Pastoral Reflections* (Norwich: Canterbury Press, 2011).

Atkinson, David and David H. Field, *New Dictionary of Christian Ethics and Pastoral Theology* (Leicester: Inter-Varsity Press, 1995).

Ballard, Paul H. (ed.), *The Foundations of Pastoral Studies and Practical Theology* (Cardiff: Board of Studies for Pastoral Studies, University College, 1986).

Ballard, Paul H. and Stephen R. Holmes, *The Bible in Pastoral Practice: Readings in the Place and Function of Scripture in the Church* (London: Darton, Longman and Todd, 2005).

Ballard, Paul H. and John Pritchard, *Practical Theology in Action: Christian Thinking in the Service of Church and Society* (London: SPCK, 2006).

Benner, David G., *Psychotherapy and the Spiritual Quest* (Grand Rapids, MI: Baker Book House, 1988).

Benner, David G., *Healing Emotional Wounds* (Grand Rapids, MI: Baker Book House, 1990).

Bobgan, Martin and Deirdre Bobgan, *The Psychological Way/The Spiritual Way* (Ada, MI: Bethany House, 1979).

Bobgan, Martin and Deirdre Bobgan, *Against 'Biblical Counseling': For the Bible* (Santa Barbara, CA: Eastgate, 1994).

Boisen, Anton T., *Out of the Depths: An Autobiographical Study of Mental Disorder and Religious Experience* (New York: Harper, 1960).

Bretherton, Luke, *Christianity and Contemporary Politics* (Chichester and Malden, MA: Wiley-Blackwell, 2010).

Bridger, Francis and David Atkinson, *Counselling in Context: Developing a Theological Framework* (London: HarperCollins, 1994).

Browning, Don S. (ed.), *Practical Theology: The Emerging Field in Theology, Church, and World* (San Francisco: Harper and Row, 1983).

Browning, Don S., *Religious Ethics and Pastoral Care* (Minneapolis, MN: Fortress Press, 1983).

Browning, Don S., *A Fundamental Practical Theology* (Minneapolis, MN: Fortress Press, 1991).

Brueggemann, Walter, *In Man We Trust: The Neglected Side of Biblical Faith* (Louisville, KY: John Knox Press, 1972).

Callahan, Annice (ed.), *Spiritualities of the Heart: Approaches to Personal Wholeness in Christian Tradition* (Mahwah, NJ: Paulist Press, 1990).

Campbell, Alastair V., *Paid to Care? The Limits of Professionalism in Pastoral Care* (London: SPCK, 1985).

Capps, Donald, *Biblical Approaches to Pastoral Counseling* (Philadelphia: Westminster Press, 1981).

Capps, Donald, *Pastoral Care and Hermeneutics* (Philadelphia: Fortress Press, 1984).

Clebsch, William A. and Charles R. Jaekle, *Pastoral Care in Historical Perspective* (New York: Jason Aronson, 1975).

Collins, Gary R., *The Rebuilding of Psychology: An Integration of Psychology and Christianity* (Wheaton, IL: Tyndale House, 1977).

Collins, Gary R., *Christian Counseling: A Comprehensive Guide* (3rd edn, Nashville, TN: Thomas Nelson, 2007).

Conn, Joann Wolski, *Spirituality and Personal Maturity* (Mahwah, NJ: Paulist Press, 1989).

Crabb, Lawrence, *Understanding People: Deep Longings for Relationship* (Grand Rapids, MI: Zondervan, 1987).

Crabb, Lawrence, *The Pressure's Off: Breaking Free from Rules and Performance* (Colorado Springs: Waterbrook Press, 2012).

Eadie, Donald, Mary Grey *et al.*, *The Faith Journey of Impaired Pilgrims* (Salisbury: Sarum College Press, 2006).

Edwards, Tilden, *Spiritual Friend: Reclaiming the Gift of Spiritual Direction* (New York: Paulist Press, 1980).

Firet, Jacob, *Dynamics of Pastoring* (Grand Rapids, MI: Eerdmans, 1986).

Ford, David F., *Self and Salvation: Being Transformed* (Cambridge: Cambridge University Press, 1999).

Ford, David F., *Christian Wisdom: Desiring God and Learning in Love* (Cambridge: Cambridge University Press, 2007).

Forrester, Duncan B., *Theology and Politics* (Oxford: Blackwell, 1988).

Fowler, James W., *Stages of Faith: The Psychology of Human Development and the Quest for Meaning* (San Francisco: HarperCollins, 1995).

Gerkin, Charles V., *Living Human Documents: Re-Visioning Pastoral Counseling in a Hermeneutical Mode* (Nashville, TN: Abingdon Press, 1984).

Goodliff, Paul, *Care in a Confused Climate: Pastoral Care and Postmodern Culture* (London, Darton, Longman and Todd, 1998).

Graham, Elaine L., *Transforming Practice: Pastoral Theology in an Age of Uncertainty* (London: Mowbray, 1996).

Graham, Elaine L., *Words Made Flesh: Writings in Pastoral and Practical Theology* (London: SCM Press, 2009).

Graham, Elaine L. and Margaret Halsey (eds), *Life Cycles: Women and Pastoral Care* (London: SPCK, 1993).

Green, Laurie, *Power to the Powerless: Theology Brought to Life* (Basingstoke: Marshall Pickering, 1987).

Green, Laurie, *Let's Do Theology: A Pastoral Cycle Resource Book* (London: Mowbray, 1990).

Grey, Mary C., *Sacred Longings: Ecofeminist Theology and Globalization* (London: SCM Press, 2003).

Guenther, Margaret, *Holy Listening: The Art of Spiritual Direction* (London: Darton, Longman and Todd, 1992).

Hughes, Selwyn, *Christ Empowered Living: Finding Stability in an Unstable World* (Farnham: CWR, 2011).

Hunt, Dave and T. A. McMahon, *The Seduction of Christianity: Spiritual Discernment in the Last Days* (Eugene, OR: Harvest House, 1985).

Hunter, Rodney J. (ed.), *Dictionary of Pastoral Care and Counseling* (Nashville, TN: Abingdon Press, 1990).

Hurding, Roger, *Roots and Shoots: A Guide to Counselling and Psychotherapy* (London: Hodder and Stoughton, 1985, 2003); published in the United States as *The Tree of Healing* (Grand Rapids, MI: Zondervan, 1988).

Hurding, Roger, *The Bible and Counselling* (London: Hodder and Stoughton, 1992).

Hurding, Roger, *Pathways to Wholeness: Pastoral Care in a Postmodern Age* (London: Hodder and Stoughton, 1998).

Jones, Stanton L. and Richard E. Butman, *Modern Psychotherapies: A Comprehensive Christian Appraisal* (Downers Grove, IL: InterVarsity Press, 1991, 2011).

Kegan, Robert, *The Evolving Self: Problem and Process in Human Development* (Cambridge, MA: Harvard University Press, 1982).

Lambourne, Robert A., *Community, Church and Healing: A Study of Some of the Corporate Aspects of the Church's Ministry to the Sick* (London: Arthur James, 1987).

Lane, Belden C., *The Solace of Fierce Landscapes: Exploring Desert and Mountain Spirituality* (Oxford: Oxford University Press, 1998).

Lartey, Emmanuel Y., *Pastoral Counselling in Inter-Cultural Perspective* (Frankfurt am Main: Peter Lang, 1987).

Lartey, Emmanuel Y., *In Living Color: An Intercultural Approach to Pastoral Care and Counseling* (London and Philadelphia: Jessica Kingsley, 2003).

Lewis, C. S., *Till We Have Faces: A Myth Retold* (London: Geoffrey Bles, 1956).

Lyall, David, *Counselling in the Pastoral and Spiritual Context* (Buckingham: Open University Press, 1995).

Lyall, David, *Integrity of Pastoral Care* (London: SPCK, 2001).

Matthews, Melvyn, *Awake to God: Explorations in the Mystical Way* (London: SPCK, 2006).

May, Rollo, *Paulus: A Personal Portrait of Paul Tillich* (London: Collins, 1974).

McFague, Sallie, *Models of God: Theology for an Ecological, Nuclear Age* (London: SCM Press, 1987).

McFague, Sallie, *The Body of God: An Ecological Theology* (London: SCM Press, 1993).

McGrath, Alister E., *A Passion for Truth: The Intellectual Coherence of Evangelicalism* (Leicester: Inter-Varsity Press, 1996).

Merton, Thomas, *Seeds of Contemplation* (2nd edn, Wheathampstead, Herts: Anthony Clarke, 1972).

Middlemiss, David, *Interpreting Charismatic Experience* (London: SCM Press, 1996).

Moon, Gary and David Benner (eds), *Spiritual Direction and the Care of Souls: A Guide to Christian Approaches and Practices* (Trowbridge: Eagle, 2004).

Moore, Zoë Bennett, *Introducing Feminist Perspectives on Pastoral Theology* (Sheffield: Sheffield Academic Press, 2002).

Nouwen, Henry J. M., *The Wounded Healer* (New York: Doubleday, 1979).

Oden, Thomas C., *Kerygma and Counseling: Toward a Covenant Ontology for Secular Psychology* (2nd edn, San Francisco: Harper and Row, 1978).

Oden, Thomas C., *Pastoral Theology: Essentials of Ministry* (San Francisco: Harper and Row, 1983).

Oden, Thomas C., *Pastoral Counsel* (New York: Crossroad, 1989).

Pattison, Stephen, *Alive and Kicking: Towards a Practical Theology of Illness and Healing* (London: SCM Press, 1989).

Pattison, Stephen, *A Critique of Pastoral Care* (2nd edn, London: SCM Press, 1993).

Pattison, Stephen, *Pastoral Care and Liberation Theology* (London: SPCK, 1997).

Pattison, Stephen, *The Challenge of Practical Theology: Selected Essays* (London: Jessica Kingsley, 2007).

Pearson, Mark, *Christian Healing: A Practical and Comprehensive Guide* (Lake Mary, FL: Charisma House, 2004).

Percy, Martyn, *The Ecclesial Canopy: Faith, Hope, Charity* (Aldershot and Burlington, VT: Ashgate, 2012).

Pietersen, Lloyd (ed.), *The Mark of the Spirit? A Charismatic Critique of the Toronto Blessing* (Exeter: Paternoster Press, 1998).

Pink, Daniel H., *A Whole New Mind: Why Right-Brainers Will Rule the Future* (London and Singapore: Marshall Cavendish, 2008).

Powlison, David, *The Biblical Counseling Movement: History and Context* (Greensboro, NC: New Growth Press, 2010).

Rakoczy, Susan (ed.), *Common Journey, Different Paths: Spiritual Direction in Cross-Cultural Perspective* (Maryknoll, NY: Orbis, 1992).

Ross, Alistair, *Counselling Skills for Church and Faith Community Workers* (Buckingham: Open University Press, 2003).

Runcorn, David, *Spirituality Workbook: A Guide for Explorers, Pilgrims and Seekers* (London: SPCK, 2006).

Runcorn, David, *Fear and Trust: God-centred Leadership* (London: SPCK, 2011).

Sanford, Agnes, *Healing Gifts of the Spirit* (Evesham: Arthur James, 1966).

Schüssler Fiorenza, Elisabeth (ed.), *Searching the Scriptures: A Feminist Introduction* (London: SCM Press, 1994).

Siang-Yang Tan, *Counseling and Psychotherapy: A Christian Perspective* (Grand Rapids, MI: Baker Academic, 2011).

Slee, Nicola, *Women's Faith Development: Patterns and Processes* (Aldershot and Burlington, VT: Ashgate, 2004).

Stange, Otto (ed.), *Pastoral Care and Context* (Amsterdam: VU University Press, 1992).

Stibbe, Mark, *Times of Refreshing: A Practical Theology of Renewal for Today* (London: HarperCollins, 1995).

Suumond, Jean-Jacques, *Word and Spirit at Play: Towards a Charismatic Theology* (London: SCM Press, 1994).

Swinton, John, *Raging with Compassion: Pastoral Responses to the Problem of Evil* (Cambridge and Grand Rapids, MI: Eerdmans, 2007).

Thornton, Martin, *Spiritual Direction: A Practical Introduction* (London: SPCK, 1984).

Tillich, Paul, *The Courage To Be* (London: Nisbet, 1952).

Tomlinson, Dave, *Re-Enchanting Christianity: Faith in an Emerging Culture* (Norwich: Canterbury Press, 2008).

Ward, Frances and Sarah Coakley (eds), *Fear and Friendship: Anglicans Engaging with Islam* (London and New York: Continuum, 2012).

Webber, Robert E., *The Younger Evangelicals: Facing the Challenge of the New World* (Grand Rapids, MI: Baker Books, 2002).

Webber, Robert E., *The Divine Embrace: Recovering the Passionate Spiritual Life* (Grand Rapids, MI: Baker Books, 2006).

Williams, E. S., *The Dark Side of Christian Counselling* (London: Wakeman Trust, 2009).

Willows, David and John Swinton, *Spiritual Dimensions of Pastoral Care: Practical Theology in a Multidisciplinary Context* (Jessica Kingsley, 2000).

Wink, Walter, *Naming the Powers: The Language of Power in the New Testament* (Philadelphia: Fortress Press, 1984).

Wink, Walter, *Unmasking the Powers: The Invisible Forces that Determine Human Existence* (Philadelphia: Fortress Press, 1986).

Woodward, James and Stephen Pattison (eds), *The Blackwell Reader in Pastoral and Practical Theology* (Oxford: Blackwell, 2000).

Wright, Tom, *Surprised by Hope* (London: SPCK, 2007).

Index of biblical references

OLD TESTAMENT

Genesis
1.27 113
16 116
16.13 117
21 116

Exodus
15.26 44
20.21 91
33.11 92
33.17–23 91
34.29 106

Deuteronomy
6.5 107
10.18 3

1 Samuel
25.3 127
25.25 127
25.33 127
25.38 127

1 Kings
19 92

2 Kings
2.9 92

Job
5.18 44
38—41 36

Psalms
19 36
23 24
34.6 85
88.16–18 37
103.2–3 44
116.7 85
139 75–6

Proverbs
1.20–21 127
2.5 127
8 141
8.27–31 126
8.30–31 36
9.10 128
12.15 127

Isaiah
40.27–31 104

Jeremiah
29.7 140

Ezekiel
47.1–12 46

Hosea
2.14 92

Zechariah
7.9–11 110

NEW TESTAMENT

Matthew
4.23 44
6.20–21 107
6.34 79
9.22 44

John
1.3–4 36
14—17 24
15.14–17 94
15.15 92

Acts
2.16 149
5.16 44
5.18–19 44
14.3 44
16.22 44
19.29–41 44

Romans
2.15 36
8.21 141
8.22–23 60
8.24–25 130
12.10 2
15.14 2

2 Corinthians
1.3–5 64
3.18 106

5.4 60
5.17 139
12.7–10 44

Galatians
1.17 92
4.4–5 90
5.14 3
6.2 2

Ephesians
1.8–9 90
4.32 2
5.21 115
6.4 136

Philippians
2.5–8 120
2.12–13 49
3.10–11 140

Colossians
1.17 36
1.26–27 89
2.13–15 57

2 Timothy
1.13 92
3.16 26

James
3.17–18 129

Index of names

Adams, Jay E. 23, 24, 25–7, 28, 29, 32, 40
Adler, Alfred 33
Allender, Dan B. 55
Anderson, Herbert 2
Anderson, Neil T. 43, 46, 48–50
Anthony of Egypt 93
Asquith, Glenn 11
Atkinson, David J. 27, 124, 151
Augsburger, David W. 1, 96
Augustine of Hippo 108

Ballard, Paul H. 10, 16
Bamber, Jonathan 123–4
Barrett, C. K. 80
Barth, Karl 78
Basil the Great 45
Baxter, Richard 88
Benner, David G. 83, 97–8, 103, 105, 108, 153
Bennett Moore, Zoë 114–15
Berkouwer, G. C 35
Bettler, John 26, 32–3
Black, David 71
Blumhardt, Johann Christoph 45
Bobgan, Deirdre 32
Bobgan, Martin 32
Boisen, Anton 10–12, 70
Bonhoeffer, Dietrich 140
Bretherton, Luke 140–1, 158
Bridger, Francis 151
Browning, Don S. 69
Brueggemann, Walter 7, 85, 92, 126, 128
Bryant, Andy 50–1, 60–1, 86–7

Bryant, Christopher 93
Bryant, Wendy 60–1

Callahan, Annice 108
Capps, Donald 84–6
Carroll, Lewis 68
Carter, John D. 29
Casey, Louise 19
Cassian, John 93
Catherine of Siena 108
Chrysostom, John 45
Clebsch, William A. 4–5, 42, 44, 45, 143
Clegg, Libby 62
Clements, Ronald E. 127–8
Coakley, Sarah 133–4
Cohen, Leonard 39
Coles, Anne 47
Coles, John 47
Collins, Gary R. 28, 32, 33, 40
Conn, Joann Wolski 80, 83, 101–3
Crabb, Larry 29, 30, 33, 34, 39, 40
Craddock, Jim 31
Cyprian 45

Dawkins, Richard 80, 152–3
De Chantal, Jane 108
Depledge, David 31
De Sales, Francis 108
Dillard, Annie 60
Dionysius the Areopagite 91
Dobson, James 39
Dooyeweerd, Herman 39

Edwards, Tilden 95
Ellis, Albert 33

Farley, Edward 9, 144
Farnsworth, Kirk E. 29
Firet, Jacob 4
Fletcher, Joseph 89
Ford, David F. 86–7, 106–7, 135–7
Fowler, James W. 153
Francis of Assisi 90, 140
Fraser, Nancy 15
Frei, Hans 76
Freud, Anna 113
Freud, Sigmund 23, 25, 33, 70, 113

Gerkin, Charles V. 12–13
Gething, Jon 123
Goodliff, Paul 151
Goss, Steve 48
Goss, Zoë 48
Graham, Elaine L. 15–16, 76, 114, 126
Green, Laurie 16–19
Gregory of Nyssa 91
Grey, Mary C. 61, 64–5, 116–17, 124–6
Grey, Nicholas 124
Guenther, Margaret 95

Hauerwas, Stanley 76
Hildegard of Bingen 45
Hiltner, Seward 10, 70–1, 143, 144
Hodge, Charles 35
Hodgett, Tina 121–3, 126, 130–1
Holmes, Arthur 36
Horney, Karen 113
Huggins, Mikail 62
Hughes, Selwyn 30, 34, 38
Hunt, Dave 55
Huxley, Aldous 80–1

Irenaeus 45, 90

Jaekle, Charles R. 4–5, 42, 44, 45, 143
James, William 144
Janzen, Waldemar 122, 127, 154, 158
John of the Cross 91
Jung, Carl 113

Kegan, Robert 79–83, 86
Kelsey, David 21, 76
Kluckhohn, Clyde 79–80
Kyle, William 71

Laing, Catriona 136–7
Lake, Frank 30, 71
Lambourne, Robert A. 71–2
Lane, Beldon 90, 93–4
Lartey, Emmanuel Y. 77–8, 119–20
Le Guin, Ursula 41
Lewis, C. S. 58, 105–6
Lindbeck, George 76
Long, Anne 104, 107
Lovelace, Richard 23, 35, 36
Loyola, Ignatius 90
Luther, Martin 45, 74, 90, 108, 140
Lyall, David 6, 8, 72
Lynch, Gordon 7, 151

McFague, Sallie 122, 157
Macfarlane, Robert 20
McGrath, Alister 34, 35, 152
McMahon, T. A. 55
MacNutt, Francis 54
Maddocks, Morris 44
Margaret Magdalen, Sister 107
Marteau, Louis 71
Maslow, Abraham 33, 98, 113
May, Rollo 74–5
Mbiti, John 80
Merton, Thomas 98–9, 108
Millbank, John 132
Miller, Elliot 49

Milne, A. A. 138
Moltmann, Jürgen 14
Moon, Gary W. 105
Morris, Colin 7–8
Mowrer, O. Hobart 25
Muir, Julia 31
Murray, Henry A. 79–80

Narramore, Bruce 28, 29, 30
Narramore, Clyde 23, 24, 28, 30, 40
Niebuhr, Richard 74
Nouwen, Henri 64, 95, 99

Oden, Thomas C. 70, 84, 143

Partridge, Trevor 30
Pattison, Stephen 5, 8, 14, 143, 149
Payne, Leanne 3, 54
Pearson, Mark 51–2, 54
Percy, Martyn 122–3, 127, 140
Perls, Frederick 113
Pickstock, Catherine 132
Pink, Daniel H. 131–2
Plotinus 91
Powlison, David 25, 26, 27, 28
Pritchard, John 10, 16
Purohit, Ramsahai 124
Pytches, David 46–7
Pytches, Mary 47

Randle, Greta 31
Rogers, Carl 23, 25, 33, 70, 79, 113
Ross, Alistair 39, 83
Runcorn, David 92, 158

Sanford, Agnes 53–4
Schaeffer, Francis 38
Schleiermacher, Friedrich 13
Schoenberg, Arnold 80

Schüssler Fiorenza, Elisabeth 116
Selby, Peter 113
Seraphim of Sarov 90
Slee, Nicola 114, 153
Smith, James K. A. 132
Sperry, Roger W. 131–2
Stapleton, Ruth Carter 52, 54
Stibbe, Mark 46
Suffield, Mervyn 31
Sweeten, Gary 38
Swinton, John 150

Taylor, Jeremy 45
Teresa, Mother 140
Teresa of Avila 91, 140
Tillich, Paul 66, 74–6, 79, 86
Tomlinson, Dave 39–40
Tracy, David 7, 76, 151
Turner, John 31

Underhill, Evelyn 89

Van Til, Cornelius 25

Walton, Heather 115–16, 117
Ward, Graham 132
Warfield, Benjamin Breckinridge 35
Weatherhead, Leslie 71
Webber, Robert E. 38–9, 89–90, 132
Wesley, John 45
Williams, E. S. 32
Wimber, John 43, 46
Wink, Walter 59–60
Winter, Richard D. 27
Wolterstorff, Nicholas 104
Woodward, James 8
Wright, Nigel 39
Wright, Tom 139, 141–2

Index of subjects

Abigail 127
abuse 15, 50, 53, 55, 115; *see also*
    violence
American Association of Christian
    Counselors 32
anger 37, 53
Anglicanism 17, 30, 60–1, 120–3
anxiety 49, 53, 75, 78–9
Association for Christian
    Counsellors 31
Association for Pastoral Care and
    Counselling 69, 72
autonomy 70, 79, 80–3

beauty 106
behaviourism 25
British and Irish Association of
    Practical Theology 9
British Association for Biblical
    Counsellors 31
British Association for Counselling
    and Psychotherapy 31
British Crime Survey 15

Calvinism 25, 35
Care and Counsel 30
case studies 11–12, 67
childhood *see* families
Christian Association for
    Psychological Studies 28, 32
Christian Counseling and
    Educational Foundation 26
church 3, 10, 43, 45–9, 57, 67,
    71, 78, 111, 122–3, 135, 140 1
clericalism 5, 11, 69, 72, 114, 144

Clinical Theology Association
    (Bridge Pastoral Foundation)
    30, 71
Cloud of Unknowing, The 91
cognition 131–2
cognitive behavioural approaches
    30, 47, 48–50, 75–6, 132
common grace 123; *see also*
    revelation, general
community 72, 76, 83, 110–13,
    121–3, 130–1
confrontation 26, 72, 128
contemplation 93, 108, 133
contract 100–1
correlation, method of 75–6,
    84, 152
counselling 12–14, 23, 53, 68, 70,
    78–9, 83–4, 94; biblical 10,
    25–40, 48, 54, 58, 67; integrational
    27–34; movement 23–4, 70,
    79, 83, 100; nouthetic 25–7;
    'spiritual' 32; *see also* pastoral
    counselling
covenant 106
creation 35, 55, 60, 86, 124, 126,
    141; new 49, 86, 141–2
creativity 61, 104, 116; *see also*
    imagination
cross, crucifixion 56–7, 76, 125,
    138–9, 140–1
culture 77–8, 82, 120–2, 124–5

David 127
defence mechanisms 101
deliverance 55–8; *see also* healing

demonology 49, 56–60, 146
dependence 75–6, 80–3, 98
depression 13, 53, 75, 100,
    118–19
Desert Fathers 93
desire 106–9, 125, 134, 137
didache 4
disability 60–2
doubt 73, 76
Dympna Centre 71

Eastern Orthodoxy 45, 73, 90,
    91, 93
ecology 123–5, 131, 139, 141
Elijah 92
embodiment 115–16, 133–4
emotion 66–7, 85
empathy 67, 131–2
eschatology 44, 47, 141–2
Eucharist 50–1, 86–7
evangelicalism 23–40, 50, 88;
    accepting 158; conservative
    25–40, 73, 133; open 73, 133;
    radical 73; 'younger evangelicals'
    39, 76, 132
evangelism 48, 120
evil 56–9, 110, 150
existentialism 74–6

faith 61, 68, 73, 74, 83, 92
families 19, 80, 82, 110–12,
    117–19, 121–2, 136–7
favouritism 37
fear 49, 54, 97, 135–7, 138
feminism 15–26, 113–14;
    ecofeminism 124–5; womanist
    114
folly 127
forgiveness 37, 54, 57, 84, 92
form criticism 84–6
Freedom in Christ ministries
    48–50, 56

friendship 92, 94, 95, 134–7
Fulcrum 34, 133

gender 11, 16, 48, 113–17, 133–4
God 41, 44, 55, 58, 68, 77–8, 98–9,
    105; as desiring 125, 134; as Father
    53, 64, 77, 90, 94; 'ground of
    being' 74–6; kingdom of 47, 56,
    74, 123, 139; as Mother 53, 77;
    as unknowable 90–1, 93–4, 106
gods 105–6
grace 56; common 35–6
Greenbelt Festival 40
grief 53, 85, 97, 104

Hagar 116–17
healer, wounded 64–5
healing, 5, 41–65, 96; anointing in
    51; charismatic 45–50; inner
    52–5; sacramental 50–2, 54
health, 43–4; *see also* wholeness
heart *see* desire
hermeneutical circle 13–14
hermeneutics 12, 19, 42, 49, 67;
    feminist 116–17; formative
    84–6; intercultural 136–7;
    soft focus 12–14, 83–4;
    of suspicion 116–17;
    'this-is-that' 46–50
Holy Spirit 22, 25, 33, 35, 40, 45,
    46–52, 59, 95, 96, 101, 106,
    131, 132, 142; baptized in 41;
    gifts of 46–7, 54
homelessness 110–12, 117–19;
    see also poverty
homosexuality 11–12, 115, 133,
    158
hope 51, 107, 125, 130, 137–42
hospitality 136, 157
humanity 74, 77, 80, 89, 96, 97–9,
    106, 108, 119–20, 126
humour 50, 63–4, 75

identity 82–3, 139
imagination 39, 54–5, 108, 131
imago Dei 97–9, 113, 120; *see also*
    humanity
incarnation 51, 56, 73, 108, 134
individualism 5, 10, 48–50, 72,
    76, 114, 132; *see also* autonomy
infertility 115–16
interculturalism 77–8, 117–21,
    124–5, 135–7
interdependence 80–3, 87, 107
intimacy 82–3, 99, 134
Islam 119, 135–7

Jehovah's Witnesses 47
Jesus Christ 25, 29, 33, 35, 36, 38,
    41, 44–5, 48, 51, 54, 59, 64, 77,
    87, 89, 92, 106–7, 138–9; as
    shepherd 68
journal-keeping 86, 104, 138
Judaism 135

kenosis 120
kerygma 4, 84
knowing, knowledge 75, 90–1,
    131–2

lament 85–6, 104; *see also* grief
liberalism 34, 73–6, 132; *see also*
    post-liberalism
listening 65, 67, 92, 107
living human documents 10–14,
    19, 77, 83
love 3, 49, 57, 77, 84, 89–90, 92,
    94, 99, 107–9, 119–21, 123, 141

magic 51, 55, 57–8, 92
male headship 115
maps, cognitive 1–2, 19–22
Mary Magdalene 116
maturation 78–83, 97;
    psychospiritual 83, 97–9, 107–9

memory 52–5
mental illness 11, 25, 60
metaphor 64, 68, 83, 90, 92–5,
    105–9, 122, 132, 140, 141
Methodism 17, 46
miracle 115
modernism 58, 59
Moses 90–1, 92, 106
multiculturalism *see* interculturalism
mysticism *see* spirituality, mystical

Nabal 127
Network Counselling and
    Training 30–1
Network of Christians in
    Psychology 31
neurosis 23, 25, 70
New Age 57–8
New Wine ministries 46–8

Operation Noah 124
orthodoxy 75; progressive 40,
    132; radical 132, 158
Oxford Christian Institute for
    Counselling 30

pain 60–1, 115, 141; *see also*
    suffering
parables 17–19, 130
paraklesis 4, 64
pastoral care 2–6, 49–51, 60–1,
    64, 68, 113, 120; definitions
    4–6, 143; shepherding role 4,
    10, 68, 143
pastoral counselling 3, 5, 12, 58,
    66–87, 99–105, 132; definitions
    68–70; *see also* counselling
pastoral cycle, spiral of care 16,
    145
pastoral theology 7–19, 70;
    feminist 114–17; *see also*
    theology, practical

patriarchalism *see* sexism
Paul 92, 106, 115, 140, 141
Pentecostalism 46, 52, 58
perfectionism 78–9
personhood 66, 79–83; *see also*
 self
pluralism 15, 43, 69, 120
politics 14–16, 125–8, 140–1
polygamy 78
post-evangelicalism 40, 76, 132
post-liberalism 73, 76–8, 132
postmodernism 38–40, 43
poverty 39, 93, 110–13, 124–5,
 141, 157
powers and authorities 57, 58–60
prayer 42, 47, 54, 56, 58, 86, 99,
 104–5, 140
praxis 7, 10, 16–19, 42, 112
pre-understanding 12–14
priesthood of all believers 69, 72
priestly paradigm 154
prophet, being a 122–3, 126,
 128–9, 140
psychiatry, psychotherapy 28, 33,
 71–2, 96, 105, 146
psychoanalysis 52, 70, 72, 144
psychology 9, 27, 28–34, 35, 48,
 52, 58, 68, 70–2

Qur'an 136

racism 60
reconciling 5
relationality 69–70, 73, 79–80, 84,
 86, 97, 98, 101, 106, 132–4, 155
resurrection 56, 116, 125, 140–2
retreats 102, 105
revelation 74, 76; general 35–6;
 special 35

salvation 73, 86–7, 125, 134, 139
Satan 25, 49, 56, 58, 84, 92

scriptural reasoning 135–7
Scripture 22, 24–7, 29, 32, 34–8,
 41, 46–9, 51, 57–8, 77
self 67, 76, 79–83, 86–7, 98–9,
 105–9, 120
self-awareness 13–14, 67, 75–6,
 88
sex 24, 50, 53, 55, 133–4
sexism 60, 113–17
silence *see* contemplation
sin 23, 25, 35, 49, 57, 58, 92;
 institutional 59
social reform 14–19, 60–1,
 110–29
solitude 92–4, 95
Soul Survivor 47
spiritual direction 5, 13, 58, 88–9,
 91–6, 99–109; desert-dweller
 92–4, 95; midwife 94–5;
 soul-friend 94, 95
spirituality 38–40, 59, 61; Catholic
 108; Celtic 88, 90; charismatic
 45–50, 58; evangelical 38–40;
 feminist 113; of the heart
 108–9; mystical 89–91; of
 presence 95–6, 103, 105
suffering 5, 11, 41–3, 50–2, 55–6,
 59, 60–1, 64, 85–7, 138
symbol 40, 48, 132, 142

theology 7–8, 72–8, 122, 132–4;
 apophatic 90–1, 93, 108;
 contemplative 133–4;
 creation 123–5; kataphatic 90;
 liberation 14, 16–19, 113–25;
 narrative 77, 115–17; practical
 8–10, 16–19
theology in response to psychology
 23–4; assimilative 23–4, 70–1;
 dialogue 24, 72; excluding 24,
 25–40, 70; integrational 24,
 27–34, 70, 71

Toronto blessing 46
tradition 132, 136
transference 101, 155
transformation 139–42
Transition Portishead 123, 131
Trinity 3, 41, 89, 90, 102, 133–4
Trinity College (Bristol) 9

unconscious 134

values 7
violence 2, 6, 15, 17, 115, 118

Westminster Pastoral Foundation 71
wholeness 77, 97, 101
wilderness 92–4
wisdom 15–16, 36, 48, 91, 94,
  126–9, 135–7
worship 85, 86, 107

ND - #0049 - 270325 - C0 - 216/138/13 - PB - 9780281070367 - Matt Lamination